I0842238

THE MILLENNIAL METROPOLIS

POWER CITIES IN THE AGE OF TRUMP

H.T. Scott Gibbons

In Memory of Guy Atlee Gibbons and Harriet Emiline Scott Gibbons

Will the circle be unbroken, bye and bye Lord, bye and bye

There's a better home awaiting, in the sky Lord, in the sky

Forward by the Author

In recent years I suddenly started to meet urban planners in various contexts in which I never had met them before. Then when working on a USAID project in the United States I was asked to conduct a review of the urban sector with respect to resilience. In the course of that work I started surveying the resources and actors involved in the urban sector and was surprised to see a number of new or expanded organizations involved particularly at the global level. These organizations were involved in setting up networks for direct interaction between cities around the world - bypassing nation states - to discuss issues of market attractiveness, business efficiency and introduction of advanced systems among others under the broad concept that "cities are the engines of economic growth".

However, these subjects of discussion do not include the basic issues of political economy or the nuts and bolts of providing jobs, income and basic services to massive and continuously growing cities. Instead, it seems that there is an economic and population management objective behind this which has not been associated with the urban sector and urban professionals before. In addition, unexpected discussion of urban issues - or rather, issues within an urban context - has become more common in magazines, newspapers, conferences and books - and among non-professionals, business interests, and policy wonks often lacking practical experience in urban management. In addition, political interests are also turning their attention to the urban sector as a key element of power in national politics. It all has a bandwagon feel to it.

As a practicing urban sector professional working on intractable problems of urban management, the things that I was reading from this new wave of urban interest did not jive with my own experience and understanding. Some, if not all topics were ultimately dangerous - pitting urban against suburban and rural citizens, for example. It seemed that many observers and commentators were promoters of an often non-transparent agenda, although possibly unwittingly.

Thankfully, some of these very people - and many others - are finally beginning to wake up and see the light. The reason for this is clear; problems that are not addressed usually do not go away and normally become worse. Global urbanization, population increase and absolute size, explosion of powerful technology, decline of the social contract, and the emergence of the vast power of the techno-managerial class have created a situation where we can no longer kick the can down the road. We as a people and as a human race must get down to work to do the demanding and necessary work of political economy and urban restructuring and management.

May 2018

Lake Victoria, Kenya

Table of Contents

The Millennial Metropolis

Power Cities in the Age of Trump

H.T. Scott Gibbons

Chapter 1 - Introduction

The title of this book should not be understood to mean that contemporary cities are made in the image of Donald J. Trump, although he is an urban man and has made some imprint on urban environments. However, the life of Donald J. Trump has coincided with the massive development and transformation of urban areas.

For decades relatively stable national settlement and political economy patterns continued even in developing countries. Major cities were at the top of the national settlement pyramid, but they were far from independent of the massive political and economic framework underneath them. There have even been recent times in both developed and less developed countries when major cities were considered to be in jeopardy from the power of the urban underclass, primary production areas, and secondary urban and rural areas. A case in point is when New York City was faced with bankruptcy and depended on the good will of the rest of the country to survive.

That bleak period of the 1970s still witnessed continued migration to cities from rural areas, especially in less developed countries, but also in developed countries. Urban areas began to present unprecedented sizes and management complexity, but secondary urban and rural areas continued to largely maintain their earlier populations and economic functions. Secondary urban areas even embarked on a period of growth. Overall, the traditional national political economic structure retained its general and apparent form.

Then, a critical mass began to be reached from the 1980s until today when not only current migration but population growth from earlier migration increased to the point where the linkage between major cities and the hinterland began to weaken. As the size of major cities increased so did the scale of their technology, management and financial structures. The disciplines related to these structures began to gravitate to and concentrate in major cities to the exclusion of other areas. This concentration altered the national economic structure by introducing total specialization in all key aspects of the economy so that secondary cities and rural areas no longer retained the economic, management and financial resources to retain their traditional role in the national hierarchy.

When combined with rapid and unstoppable globalist restructuring, and massive redistribution to the power elite and techno-managerial elite of global and national wealth, a new environment emerged where an increasingly small number of major cities began to assert their newly created interests and power over all others through the techno-managerial elite. These are the power cities of the technology control era, coincidentally the Age of Trump, and their structure and function can be called the millennial metropolis.

This book seeks to understand this new environment in detail and consider its impact on nearly all aspects of human life and interaction. In addition, it presents likely challenges and potential outcomes that may result from trends and developments already too far progressed to be re-oriented. This book principally addresses urbanization, political economy and technology, although it necessarily addresses other subjects, most particularly economic justice. This book seeks primarily to explore the relationship of political economy with global urbanization, and the related options for social and physical organization.

For the purposes of this book, the Age of Trump is considered to be Donald Trump's personal second or third coming - not as in his The Art of the Deal or "The Apprentice" - but as a new and unexpected standard bearer of the circumvented or manipulated classes in the new political economy struggle in the United States which came to the fore in the American Presidential Campaign of 2016. The underlying struggle had been at work for some time before that, certainly since 2007 and possibly as far back as the early 1960s, but

2016 can be considered as a useful cutoff date, because suddenly, massive numbers of voters in the United States found that traditional structures, institutions and leaders no longer represented them and that they had been circumvented and dispossessed.

Whatever the original heart of heart reasons for his candidacy, Donald Trump was himself also made by underlying and emerging conditions even more than by events. Around the world, similar conditions have generated movements, until now mainly sub-national and without any significant and charismatic leaders like Donald Trump, that are challenging similar structures, institutions and social contracts. The result is two massive interest camps within the political economy - one that desires techno-managerial control by a limited number of the self-selected, and another that is essentially a revanchist opposition that wishes to push back the recent order, but without any well developed or articulated plan of action.

The emergence of this second camp has placed at risk the vast majority of political and economic assumptions and investments of the techno-managerial class. Surprisingly, the impact of this second camp may be greatest on the ambitions of China, which has relied on the assumption of global statist control to implement its ambition of creating a new and independent global trading system centered on Peking. The stakes could not be higher. Strangely, the current situation resembles both the Bolshevik Revolution and also the fall of the USSR. The dreams of many and the fears of the other many are at stake and the outcome can accommodate little compromise.

The power cities that have emerged are the homes of the power elite and their agents, the techno-managerial elite. These power cities dominate secondary cities and towns, the hinterlands, and now even seek to dominate cities in other countries. The power gap between and within the power cities and the rest is unsustainable and is creating social conflict which will have to be resolved. There are four possible future scenarios for management of global urbanization, particularly in the case of the United States. None of them are fully satisfactory to current political economy ideologies. All of them indicate reduced freedom for most people, but one of them is more attractive in its potential to reduce social conflict. It is the Millennial Metropolis Model (MMM). It replaces the currently discussed alternative of universal basic income with a more fundamental universal basic services approach that requires a more comprehensive and activist urban and regional planning program.

Chapter 2 - The Techno-Managerial Class

The Grand Social Coalition and the Middle Class Society

The Age of Trump has been in the making for decades and it has to do with changes in human settlement patterns (urbanization) as well as political economy. In the case of the United States the most important characteristics of this age are the massive growth, urbanization and mobility of the world population, the decline of the middle class and the dramatic rise to power of the techno-managerial elite and the super-rich power elite. Poverty and lack of equal access have been popular urban issues for a long time. However, fundamental structural issues of political economy have rarely been raised in the urban context. Now urban areas are emerging as the battlefields for national struggles to dominate and control the new political economy. It is that struggle that will determine the function and form of urban areas in the years to come.

In my book, <u>Trapped by History</u>, I presented the complex changing character of socio-economic elites vis-a-vis the middle class in the United States. The key findings from that analysis are related to those to those presented in Thomas Piketty's <u>Capital in the 21st Century</u>, and in Charles Murray's <u>Coming Apart</u>. Piketty documents how in earlier times elites derived their wealth and income from land or physical assets, lost this wealth due to World War I, the Great Depression and World War II, and in the new economy have hitched a ride to their own restoration through control of management with no connection to fixed assets of place.

Murray takes a different approach to analysis of the same situation from a sociological perspective. Murray presents a picture where in the past elites were somehow bound to the rest of the population, but became aliened from physical place primarily through social and cultural segregation.

As both of those authors explain, elites were limited by the earlier structure at least until the 1960-70 period. Then suddenly something changed. In recent times a techno-managerial elite has emerged which derives its status from management, regulation and technical structures, and which serves a resurgent power elite that dominates through finance rather than investment in localized physical assets.

As observed by Murray Bookchin, feudal, mercantilist and capitalist structures functioned contemporaneously, even as additional trading and industrial elites and then a much larger middle class emerged. The industrial elite was much greater and often had more power and influence than the earlier trading and landed elites. However, the industrial elite continued to be generally bound to local areas and communities, as well as to the broad middle class in a political economy structure that reached its zenith in the United States and which prevented that elite from gaining controlling dominance. From time to time there were examples, such as the robber barons in the United States, where the elite did exert substantial independent power over the political economy, but there was usually pushback against this and it did not seem to be sustained.

For much of the 20th Century labor made substantial progress within the political economy and the majority of labor joined the middle class and the grand industrial-era economic coalition. This grand coalition resulted in a broad national stability in the United States that was threatened only by extreme ideologues, a small underclass and the Cold War communist bloc. In <u>Trapped by History</u>, I reference a number of factors such as the anomalous world political economy after World War II that created conditions that allowed a new elite, the techno-managerial class, to emerge, and to quietly and invisibly strengthen and free itself from the social, cultural and geographical controls that undergirded the grand coalition.

Restructuring of the Grand Social Coalition

By the end of the 20th Century extreme ideology and Cold War threats had apparently faded away, leaving only the underclass as a threat to the grand coalition, giving birth to the unprecedented hubris represented by Francis Fukuyama in his book, <u>The End of History</u>. Over years the historical underclass had been pacified at a level that provided relative peace in the society, but the cost of which continuously increased and was not fully accepted by a large part of the society. However, the new techno-managerial class championed this social buy off and increasingly shifted its cost to the middle class facilitated by increasingly favorable economic conditions. The techno-managerial class also supported development assistance to less developed countries and increased immigration in the guise of sharing opportunities and wealth - but that class participated less and less in the cost of that buy-off and sharing, and more and more in its benefits. After the end of the Cold War the techno-managerial class added to this buy-off and sharing structure an unquestioned promotion of globalization to enrich footloose capital and partner elites in less developed countries (as emphasized by the Latin American dependency theorists).

All these changes represented a betrayal by the techno-managerial class of the national grand coalition, and the establishment of a new coalition of everyone but the historical middle class in the United States - but without a repudiation of the grand coalition. As a result, many members of the middle class still continued to believe that they shared some economic, social and cultural interests with the techno-managerial class, despite their growing doubts about their status in the emerging political economy. In fact, the techno-managerial class rose to be the dominant power in the United States (and also in almost every other country) with a declining need for middle class support. This declining need was achieved because of the miraculous explosion of market consumption from the middle class that masked its declining political and economic power. This market consumption was largely due to the manipulation by the techno-managerial elite of currency exchange rates to keep prices low, to the introduction and massive expansion of future-mortgaging credit, and to the normalization of two-income households. This market consumption system required a global production and distribution system, as well as economies of massive scale. In order to make this a success, it was necessary to transfer technology, knowledge and consumption to less-developed countries, and to financialize the economy.

A consequence of this new system was the replacement of many of the native-born American middle class in emerging professions by immigrants in the United States and by domestic labor in other countries. That resulted in increased wages, profits and political payoffs for operations in less developed countries, while at the same time reducing native-born middle class wealth, upward mobility and small business profits in the United States. This began a cycle where income and consumption was transferred from the American middle class to an increasing proportion of the population in less-developed countries and to those who emigrated from those countries. As production and wealth were transferred to less developed countries, new opportunities were created for hiding profits generated by foreign operations, and substantial new demand arose for all classes of assets and products that would ultimately compete with that of the United States and other developed countries and result in higher prices and lower standards of living there. This is part of the reason why returns on productive (as opposed to speculative and intellectual property) investments have been steadily decreasing.

An initial weakness of the techno-managerial class was that it broadly shared with the middle class the common national financial and regulatory systems, which were directly felt in daily life and were difficult to change stealthily. However, financial regulation of institutions that was controlled by the techno-managerial elite had been reduced for many years, greatly increasing the profitability of financial activities for the techno-managerial class. By the turn of the 21st Century deregulation made it more possible to de-link local savings from local investment and control, and even to distort the nature and authenticity of financial records, draining resources from communities into the national and international financial system where there was greater opportunity for malfeasance. In the aftermath of 9-11, increased controls and charges on routine financial transactions was mainly targeted at and further weakened the middle class.

But it was the regulatory changes after the financial turmoil of the Great Recession which introduced stealth currency de-valuation that finally put the nails in the coffin of - and subdued - the middle class. This de-valuation was achieved by reducing the value of savings through low interest rates set by the Federal Reserve and the facilitation of various high level financial transactions by the techno-managerial class that provided higher rates of return to them than those available to the middle class. This resulted in the enrichment of the techno-managerial class and opportunities for it to acquire more power over the middle class.

The emergence of the techno-managerial class was made possible by fundamental changes in the political economy which we can consider as a loosening of public and private, formal and informal controls over that class. This loosening was a Janus-faced development in that it provided advantages and benefits to the techno-managerial class to transcend restrictions of the political economy - but at the same time required introduction of compensatory and balancing restrictions on the middle class. At the same time as controls on moving capital across jurisdictions were removed and public subsidies increased for the techno-managerial class, increased and unsubsidized individual educational, professional, liability and technical standards were imposed on the middle class.

The techno-managerial class had managed to grow regulation over the years to the point that only that class or individuals sponsored by it could qualify or bear the cost of participation in a wide range of economic activities largely due to large scales of economy which the techno-managerial class supported. Examples of that regulation include the systems of college education and professional accreditation. Admission to and funding for the most prestigious colleges is now more readily available for the favored non-native and non-middle classes in comparison with the native-born middle class. In contrast, the elite have powerful networks that allow them to avoid the need to compete for college admission and for investment in accreditation.

It was with the capture and manipulation of financial and regulatory systems that the techno-managerial class reached a stage where it was accountable to no one and to no place, and where it could set all the rules. It is still curious that the Great American Middle Class did not resist these efforts by the techno-managerial elite. In my book, <u>Trapped by History</u>, I address this mystery. The reason for the lack of resistance, is in brief, that in addition to the escape of the techno-managerial class from dependence on the Great American Middle Class, communities and local jurisdictions, the Great American Middle Class has been dismembered into a number of interest groups, such as race, gender, language, age, etc. whose individual priority interests now outweigh their common interests.

In addition, in a short period of time, the techno-managerial class has grown as a significant number of the Great American Middle Class have joined it, and at the same time as a similar significant number of the Great American Middle Class have declined into a rootless labor class. As a result, there is no longer a natural un-fragmented Great American Middle Class voting bloc that can oppose the techno-managerial class. Moreover, the Great American Middle Class has been indoctrinated for decades to believe that science, technology, management and so-called merit, as represented and performed by the techno-managerial class, are in their best interests, objective, and prosperity/equity-providing.

As a result of these changes local, regional and national political economies have been superseded in favor of a global scale political economy. With this change the number of economic playing fields of the power elite has been reduced while the scale of their power and wealth has increased dramatically. At the same time, new subordinate levels of global political economy management have emerged. This has resulted in a worldwide increase in the techno-managerial class with members who range from the mildly to the shockingly prosperous. However, this class is not the power elite, but it operates a system that facilitates its status and activities as well as those of the much smaller power elite.

Nevertheless, members of the techno-managerial class may have influence far beyond their personal circles. This class can include individuals ranging from university professors, consulting engineers, actors, journalists and religious leaders to famous individuals, corporate directors, etc. Although the difference in wealth and influence among these individuals can be very great, they are all members of the techno-managerial class, although they are rewarded unequally based on the networking, importance and difficulty of their respective roles in managing the political economy.

It is important to understand that the techno-managerial class is a new class. While the brief Post-World War II middle class was a partial descendent of the late industrial-era middle class with an independent interest in opposition to the power elite and the underclass, the techno-managerial class serves to manage a political economy that includes a public administration and regulation system, a media-entertainment-education propaganda structure and a military-security-industrial-consumption complex that converges with the interests of a small power elite - mainly because of its financial resources, with the underclass and with their counterparts in other countries against the increasingly disempowered and isolated middle class.

It is unclear exactly why the techno-managerial class has allied with these other classes against the Great American Middle Class. It is possible that the power elite has so much wealth and controls sufficient structures that the techno-managerial class is powerless to reform or replace those key elements of the political economy that satisfy the power elite. More cynically it could be that the techno-managerial elite has been morally corrupted to the point that it no longer opposes the function of the power elite - but rather now wishes to capture or share that role.

The techno-managerial class has also allied itself with the under and disempowered labor class - a class that has traditionally opposed similar elite classes - against the great middle class. In this there may be some parallel with the Soviet Union elite that sustained and marshaled the labor class to make its privileged position possible, although there was no opposing middle class there. In the current environment, the techno-managerial class can be seen using the underclass as its agents in the volunteer army, the TSA, the government sector, and much of the service sector, in addition to criminal, subversive and civil disturbance activities. The role of the underclass established by the techno-managerial class in this broad range of activities serves to undermine the social, cultural, political and economic status of the middle class by removing any middle class control over those activities and by establishing independent administrative authority over, and disrespect for, the great middle class.

Segregation of the Techno-Managerial Class from the Commons

The global techno-managerial class is increasingly rapidly segregating itself from the bulk of the world's population at every geographical and jurisdictional level in terms of micro as well as relative location, public/common services and market consumption. This segregation facilitates the withdrawal of the techno-managerial class from general participation and public financial contribution even as it has gained a massive wealth transfer from the middle class. This is one of the key reasons why the quality of public services of previous times is no longer possible. The withdrawal of the techno-managerial class from a broad range of public shared services or market functions also allows the techno-managerial class to avoid the need to interact with its underclass agents as well as with the ordinary middle class, making it possible for the underclass to be used as a direct agent to enforce the techno-managerial power against the middle class.

The techno-managerial class facilitates vast social and economic segregation through various regulations and structures and is rewarded with comfortable positions in the society, and secure jobs in the education, government, corporate and entertainment sectors. The primary job of the techno-managerial class is to exempt the power elite and themselves from public accountability and oversight. The result is the increasing concentration of those classes in a limited number of cities around the world where they organize national and global political economies according to their interests.

The techno-managerial class generally provides no primary wealth generation capacity other than management control from which it extracts commissions. Although the power elite are great beneficiaries of the current political economy this does not mean that they can impose or manage it at the overall system level, even though they may have conceived and promoted it. It is the techno-managerial class that implements all aspects of the middle class-destroying political economy for its own management-commission gain, leaving the greatest benefits to the power elite, even though in addition to self-interest its members may think that they are expanding and enforcing a self-initiated preferred social contract.

Chapter 3 - The Techno-Managerial Class and Modern Governance

The function of the techno-managerial class requires a diminishing number of people as the power level increases, especially in the political sector. This can be seen in the more or less stable number of elected officials at the national level even as overall populations and economies explode. The result of this is the increased power of the highest positions in all countries. Although Moses Naim in his book, <u>The End of Power</u>, makes many valid and interesting observations that he uses to conclude that various aspects of power have declined in recent times, I would argue that it is not power itself that has declined, but that sometimes the specific individual 'users' of power and some specific 'combinations' or 'contexts' of power that 'appear' to have declined.

An example of this new form of power can be seen in the recent action by the United States Federal Communications Commission to dramatically alter the rules of Internet regulation (which may ultimately have an impact on the Internet of Things - IoT - and smart city programs). In that decision the FCC has administrative power that can essentially not be influenced by the public. However, its jurisdiction is constrained so while it allows the freedom of providers to accept more influence by paying interests, it cannot totally block access and expression by non-paying interests or non-commercial providers. As such, the impact of the commission is limited in comparison with the power of the commission in the 1950s when communications were more concentrated, but its power is larger in the number of affected persons and impact today. Moreover, if public opposition or scandal brings the FCC or the Chairman into disrepute, they may be forced to step down, but the ruling is almost certain to remain beyond their individual tenures.

At the state level the pattern of techno-managerial elites of the national level is broadly replicated. However, the power level diminishes because substantial power and financial resources have already been expropriated by the national government before they reach the state level. State and county boundaries are generally stable like national boundaries, although in less developed countries these also change with population size. However, at lower levels such as district and ward, boundaries are less stable even in developed countries. The prevailing structure of national, state and local governance presents growing demands at lower levels of government with increased numbers of the techno-managerial class, but with less adequate and buoyant resources, while national government also enjoys increased numbers of the techno-managerial class, but *with* buoyant revenues as well as umbrella control over the increasing overall population.

In countries like the United States where government legitimacy originated at the local level rather than the national level, significant resources have historically been controlled by local elected officials, making local government activities still attractive to many and reducing the desire for competition at the national level. However, since the national government imposes increased standards on local government, the adequacy of local revenue in local governance has decreased, stimulating greater interest in state and national government activities where the number of power opportunities has remained mostly fixed. This is one aspect of what Peter Turchin has described as an excess supply of elites. However, it is not necessarily that there is an overall excess supply of elites, but that the given supply is increasingly focused and concentrated. When faced with the limitations of ordinary cities, ambitious members of the techno-managerial class gravitate to the upper hierarchy of government, business and technology management in power cities.

Chapter 4 - The Pyrrhic Victory of Devolution

In developing countries, particularly former colonies, urban local governments have not had significant revenues in recent times, so local elites have always looked to state and national levels of government for personal and public revenues. As a result, there were more people interested in state and national politics than could be accommodated within the decision-making and spoils-distribution activities. As a result, many countries have implemented devolution policies with the objective of re-directing the attention of as many elites as possible away from the national and state governments to the local level. However, this has come at a time when increased revenue and administrative control is at the national level, but where increased urban services and amenities are required at the local level. This has created a conflict which needs resolution.

The legacy of centralized government administration at the national and state levels is still felt strongly in most less developed countries despite attempts at devolution. However, even where devolution has been implemented according to plan, there are still major administrative and financial gaps due to the nature of devolution as commonly practiced and the emerging challenges of modern urban local governance.

Devolution as a term has a narrow scope although there is a powerful association with its linguistic evolution. Literally it suggests a slightly negative concept of decline or reduction, but popular recent use has been of a specific concept of less than complete transfer of power from one government to another, usually implying a granting of specific powers from a primary government to a subsidiary one, especially in areas of historical British influence. Some have praised the concept of devolution as a useful form of government and political management in a world of large institutional government. From that one might imagine that devolution is a positive response to the public demand for self-rule and local control of resources. Indeed, devolution should inherently provide those two results. However, the outcomes are often more apparent than real.

Briefly, let's examine the promised devolution results of self-rule and local ownership of resources. Self-rule is not self-determination or independence, but a delegation of some powers from total powers. In practice, in countries like India, Pakistan, Sri Lanka, Iraq, Nigeria, Kenya, etc. where this has been or is being implemented, it has involved a grant of secondary powers still subject to central guidance and standards, but without significant resources for implementation. How can this be? Largely the practical situation is to assign or devolve 'responsibilities' that are usually significantly greater than those currently implemented by local government along with declining subsidies and the exhortation to increase local revenues which had remained stagnant prior to devolution. In short, this means the expectation of increased local performance, but along with the challenge of increasing local revenues.

Under normal national practice the central government collects national economy revenues and distributes these to local governments according to some formula, but sometimes also by caprice. Under devolution, distributed revenues are normally initially increased while local governments adjust to increased responsibilities/expectations and then central transfers are gradually reduced in the expectation of improved local revenue generation. The central government almost always retains current and buoyant core revenues for itself and uses only a small portion of these for the declining revenue transfers given in support of devolution. Shares in national wealth such as primate city activity, import duties, natural resources, etc. are not devolved. Local governments must rely mainly on revenues such as property and sales taxes, which are politically difficult to increase.

As a result, it is difficult for self-rule to be achieved because of incomplete powers, resources and revenues, and greatly increased local public attention, expectation and demand. In short, pressures - not rewards - of devolution are hived off to local governments, actually weakening them vis-à-vis the central government. In this situation, local officials face pressure from all sides locally so that they do not have the leisure to continue their struggle at higher levels of 'court' government which remain the preserve of the more limited and privileged power elite. Of course, devolution is still in the broadly experimental stage, but we can at least look at the experience of Pakistan, for example, to see the rejection of the blatant use of devolution to divert the attention of local elites away from the national level.

In addition to so-called self-rule, devolution also suggests local ownership of resources. In countries like Iraq where natural resources are not uniformly distributed throughout the country, any devolution of natural resources is highly disruptive since it naturally replaces 'national' 'shared' resources with unequal 'natural' local resources. As a result, demands for devolution of power in an environment of unequal natural resources within an existing country are difficult to justify practically because they are based on the principle of 'locality'. The ultimate locality is the individual himself so the application of devolution principles would easily extend logically to supporting local urban-rural and even individual property disparities. As a result, there have not been many successful examples of this being implemented in the modern era, although radical Ayn Randian free market and individualism advocates supporting total locality have been attracting more attention in recent years.

Devolution is usually granted without major street protests. When there are street protests the result is usually independence or crackdowns. Devolution is often initiated by the central government itself as a political relief valve. Justification for this can be the increase in population scale or geographic coverage, but even then in cases like South Sudan, the available resources are not sufficient to justify innumerable devolved local governments. Since central governments have a poor record of administering local governments so they often wish to rid themselves of this responsibility. However, defense and national security responsibilities are retained and in practice allow the central government to exert its power over local governments as it wishes; a situation that we have seen recently in Catalan, Spain.

The situation in the United States is not directly comparable to this since the country's origin was in a confederation of sub-national state governments, and a structure of apparent self-rule still remains there. However, most of the same counter-intuitive results seen under devolution have slowly been obtained through stealth in the United States as well; largely though environmental, safety, labor and professional regulations and costs imposed on local governments. Going forward this will result in increasing power and wealth disparities and inequities within the nation as power cities ally with central governments to harvest the first fruits. Most local governments will eventually reject this hand me down world.

Chapter 5 - The Power City and the Rest

The Historical Relationship Between the City and Country

It was only in recent times that urban sector issues were collected in the discipline of city planning. The original discipline of city planning was established in a time of great future optimism and included physical and social aspects, although political economy aspects were given less consideration. Prior to this the broader urban environment was the domain of architects, large institutions, the military and the police. Cities had emerged as a key component in the ascent of man and civilization, largely as the result of development of specialized skills, government and management of resources. The emergence of cities meant that a mass of people living in a concentrated area produced advanced products and activities supported by lower valued food and raw materials from rural areas. Better organization, technology and power allowed cities to extract these from the country until there was revolt. More of the products of cities were used within the cities than in rural areas so the terms of exchange always had to be more favorable for the city.

That meant that the balance between city and countryside was more or less predictable; the city could only maintain the required specialized workers and other labor that could be supported by excess rural production. There are only two ways to generate excess rural production: exchange of specialized products and involuntary exaction. Rural production was historically limited by extent of land and supply of labor. Extent of land area was largely determined by the ability of the organization in the city to provide the military force to control, protect and possess land area to the exclusion of other cities and to exert its terms of trade on the residents therein. Supply of labor depended on the reproduction and health of the native population, and often on the import of additional labor from outside the region of city control - or redeployment of excess urban population to the countryside.

So it was generally each city's rural hinterland that was the limiting factor on cities. Of course with the production of specialized products and services, trade and cultural relations with other cities also developed. But it was the rural engine of each city that powered it in those relations. In different eras and places relations between city and country developed unique aspects. Feudal systems allowed owners of the countryside to control rural labor and sometimes to establish themselves as both landlords and city elite or vice versa. Sometimes the city powers directly pillaged the country population almost to the point of destroying the very production that drove the city. From time to time nomadic forces pillaged the countryside and later sacked the cities as a result of that chokehold. Only on rare occasions did desperate country people threaten the city.

The early control of the countryside by the city was through resort to military force. Over centuries this became institutionalized into feudal relations which were a type of improvement, and later to the yeoman farmer structure which provided more individual independence and some increased prosperity. The yeoman farmer structure began to decline as the nature of rural products and production, and the terms of exchange with the city changed. Increasing importance of large scale mechanized farming operations, and later encroachment of urban activities far into the countryside have largely eliminated the yeoman farmer. What remains in the countryside now is limited subsistence farming, hobby farming, small town market assembly of produce, lower cost residential and manufacturing locations, and of course the large scale modern agricultural economy controlled by urban powers and with vastly reduced labor inputs.

The Emergence of Power Cities

What replaced the historical agricultural countryside as a resource check on powerful cities in a few short decades were secondary and third tier cities, and less urbanized regions. Like the situation in the past, the power cities continue to provide the military control and protection of these areas - when it suits them. Now power cities do not merely control the hinterland; they own it. However, unlike in the past, this time there is diminishing need for its people as labor, except perhaps in the military, security and population management services. The people of second and third tier cities also rely on rural products - now owned by power cities; as well as on primary production and financial services in power cities. Unlike the agricultural country people of the past, the people of the second and third tier cities have very little to trade in exchange for their needs from the power city.

This weakness in the physical trading relationship between power cities and their hinterland is compounded by the total control of the financial relations by the power cities. The residents of second and third tier cities can be considered as legacy population and refugees from an eclipsed rural economy. Accordingly, the economic resources of those areas can be considered as a type of severance pay from the power city financial system to cover the maintenance of their residual historical populations, rather than as a payment for a current exchange of goods and services. As the power cities have taken control over the hinterland economy and financial systems, their reach can extend beyond that conceived in von Thünen's central place theory because the boundary between producer and consumer has blurred. As communications and entertainment services have centralized in production and expanded in their transmission, the area of influence of power cities has also increased culturally and politically. As Charles Murray has observed in Coming Apart, power elites and their technocrat agents are increasingly drawn to the power city magnet, making it unlikely that influencers will originate or remain in second and third tier cities.

Numerous recent articles and studies contain observations that the trend of gentrification and concentration of power in power cities is reversing or declining, but this is not correct. The factual situation of increasing development and dominance of a global system of power cities is undeniable, although it can be misrepresented in a number of ways through the clever use of definitions and boundaries. However, Charles Murray's <u>Coming Apart</u> and other books that reference United States zip codes, and visual inspection show that the trend of power concentration is clear and undiminished.

It is only the political structures of the past, reflecting a brief historical flirtation with mass political representation, that preserve some political economy participation and representation of areas beyond the power cities. That means that without production, economic, financial or propaganda power, these hinterland areas are becoming only population to be controlled and manipulated. With the near universal faux-democratic political structures that emerged around the world in the 20th Century, this new political economy structure reduces the independent political power in the hinterland in favor of developing it as a second playing field for battles within the power cities themselves. In this cynical view, power cities have power elite struggles that can be expanded to the hinterland where they are fought on the basis of the larger population numbers there. As a result, under a faux-democratic system the hinterland population can counter the results of any competition *within* a power city, but on the terms dictated by the power city and not with an independent influence from the interests of the hinterland.

Chapter 6 - The Nature of Power Cities

The Impact of Non-Spatial Influence

In developed countries several cities together may function as a single power city or power capital through control of communications, regulations and technology; adding a complexity to central place theory which von Thünen could not have anticipated, while in less developed countries single cities are generally - but not always - both power city and power capital.

Given this new structure of political economy there are two questions to be asked: what are the natural limits of power city influence and what is the nature of conflict between and within the power cities. When the power of one city has been extended it begins to meet resistance from that of other cities as observed by von Thünen for traditional economies. This has traditionally been accepted as the natural limitation of city influence. However, von Thünen could not anticipate the revolutionary impact of non-spatial influence that would emerge with increasing frequency in the techno-managerial age.

Non-spatial influence is the result of modern sophisticated communications, propaganda, education, and technology, regulatory and financial systems control. These non-spatial influence components have introduced two new complications to central place theory: *joint-power cities and control agent cities.* Joint-power cities are characterized by divided control of separate elements of a common political economy. This can be seen in the United States in the division of government, entertainment, business, technology, energy and commodities broadly among the cities of Washington, Los Angeles, New York, San Francisco, Houston and Chicago for example.

These cities have their own special area within the political economy, but are totally interrelated so that they function as joint-power cities. That means that a single system has multiple nodes rather than a single von Thünen node. This makes for a very powerful structure since it combines all aspects of a political economy and allows all joint-power cities to have nearly equal benefits. The nature of central place power and political economy control means that all other areas are controlled by the system managed by the joint-power cities. As a result, the joint-power cities control the non-joint power cities as well as their individual central place systems. The difference between the classical central place structure and the joint-power city structure is that the central place structure was hierarchical with an origin and an extremity, while the joint-power city structure is an overarching system imposed on top of that spatial structure to dominate the system.

Control agent cities are similar to central place cities. However, their attraction power based on distance is mainly derived from legacy conditions from an earlier economy. Their fundamental power is their location and resources for political economy system administration on behalf of power cities. This is performed as assembly, collection and administration centers oriented to traditional von Thünen spatial functions - but they themselves have no real independent power. In the United States these can be represented even by otherwise important cities such as Philadelphia, Atlanta, Boston, and smaller urban centers such as Charlotte, Miami, Nashville, Minneapolis, etc. In other countries these functions are normally performed by capital or business cities. The main difference between the system of control agent cities and the von Thünen central place system is that modern political economy requires a minimum threshold of administrative and economic power for the function of control agent cities. As a result, lesser settlements increasingly cease to be central places, since modern communication, regulation and technology economies no longer conform to legacy boundaries even at the national level. As a result, power cities and control agent cities now make claims on areas based on, but beyond their legacy boundaries.

The Power City and the Nation State

Within the nation state the power city is a challenge to the traditional structure of non-coercive political economy, since the local economy and political structure were connected and represented in a hierarchy from homestead to village to town to city. With the removal of the lower tiers of settlement from this system, and with the super-imposition of the power city structure over the remaining central place system, the largest area and extensive population - the so-called 'fly-over country' - has become excluded from power in the modern political economy.

As long as the nation state structure functioned effectively, conflicting claims of influence at the international level could be resolved either by agreements or by military conflict. When power cities are also national capital power cities this can still be the case since the political economy allows the capital power city to control the military that is largely recruited from the powerless hinterland. Resolution of conflicting claims by capital power cities can be achieved in a manner similar to the practice in the late Ottoman Turkey state, in European colonies and in Post-World War II developing countries where powerful nations demanded special legal and administrative arrangements for their citizens residing and operating in weaker countries. Capital power cities also have some leverage over non-capital power cities through their capital cities, although complications can arise there as well. However, when power cities are not capital power cities, achieving successful influence outside their legacy national boundaries presents challenges.

That challenging situation, which has very limited recent historical precedent, is where the influence of a non-capital power city is on non-capital city or on a capital city in another country. Where influence from a capital power city in one country is on a capital of another country it is possible to organize a functional arrangement similar to that of power cities over their national hinterland, but with the added conflict with another nation's policies and interests. An example of this might be current Chinese relationships with various countries. However, when a non-capital power city seeks to exert influence over a capital city (and by extension, over the entire nation), such as that of New York over some Latin American countries, this requires more effort and additional coordination with the capital power city. When a power city of either type seeks to exert influence over a non-capital city in another country, it inevitably must bypass or reduce the authority of that country's capital city. An example might be that of San Francisco (Silicon Valley) and Bangalore, India; or that of numerous textile industry cities with Special Economic Zones around the world; or even of numerous cities with major tourist centers. The main conflict in this situation is within the affected country. Until now this has been addressed largely through corruption, and there has been no significant political empowerment of the non-capital cities vis-à-vis their associated nation states. However, there are a number of power cities such as London, that are leading efforts to create political economic independence from either their capital power cities, or from their associated nation states themselves.

As the techno-managerial economy grows, there are an increasing number of power non-capital cities, and growth of direct influence paths between them. As a result sub-national power city elites chaff at national and sub-national restrictions. One way of circumventing these restrictions has been by setting up special economy zones (SEZ) that function to alienate local resources for non-local interests and without local control. Development of that economic model has been under way for several decades now. However, this model was largely based on the labor-intensive manufacturing economy whose importance is in long term decline.

The emerging technological administrative economy has established its base in power city CBDs which cannot be alienated from the other parts of their associated power cities. Instead of low-cost and low-skilled labor, this economy, whose definition still needs attention, is populated by the creative class, as Richard Florida as named it. This creative class is not necessarily a power class, although those who control it do have power. This class in its broadest and less flattering extent includes increasing numbers of millennials, immigrants, footloose labor, non-traditional families, non-property-owners, minorities (although not all) and general misfits. These are not only the small group of IT and AI geniuses, but are mainly powerless day laborers and sharing economy serfs. Many are refugees from the failing second and third tier cities who are relocating to the power cities in order to share in the new restructured economy.

Within the power cities there is a hierarchy of residents. There are the power elites, the techno-managerial elite, the creative class, the residual middle class and the labor class. Only a small portion of the residents of power cities have economic independence and security. The broad creative class generally has few physical assets, and a planning horizon based on current income. As a result, it is both able and compelled to seek and take advantage of economic opportunities no matter where they may be. This means that it has few loyalties and values beyond current survival and self-gratification.

Since its members have reduced possessions, community connections, and intergenerational future orientation they can enjoy a comfortable mode of living which can potentially be replicated in almost any urban environment. The main characteristic of this class is its desire for efficient and limited-commitment living arrangements. These can be, but often are not, provided everywhere. So even if there is a power elite and techno-managerial elite in the city, it appears that economic opportunities need to be combined with this type of living environment to also attract the creative class.

The middle and labor classes are attracted by the underlying economic activity and location is less a matter of choice than of available affordability. In another time they would have remained in the hinterland with a sustainable standard of living, but as that alternative has been rapidly foreclosed, many of them are relocating to the power cities. Unfortunately, the power city urban standard of living is too high to provide to all its denizens - especially in the developing world.

By the time of the 2016 Brexit Referendum and United States Presidential Election a handful of power cities had acquired almost definitive dominance over their hinterlands (and even nation-states) and were seeking to define themselves with respect to other power cities at home and abroad. Then suddenly, to the surprise of almost everyone, the power cities were rebuffed and the hinterlands spoke. It was a voice without words, but the message was clear. The people of the hinterland were still alive, present in significant numbers and did not want to be dominated by the power cities. Almost as suddenly came the reaction from the power cities - we don't need your blessing or voluntary support, we can survive with our other power city friends in the brave new world - but is it true?

The Emergence of the Millennial Metropolis

In recent decades the share of world population has shifted substantially from rural to urban. The large populations previously needed to harvest and extract natural resources have been greatly reduced with the result that trade, not production, now defines the nature of the city with all other places. Cities, or more appropriately, their urban people, are beginning to have more in common with other cities than with their hinterlands, especially with the tremendous global population mobility that creates urban populations that have no connection with the adjacent hinterlands.

Present nation states are the historical result of natural features, common culture, and primary supply chains for basic goods and products that could be managed under a common polity. Until recently the larger size and resources of the countryside meant that significant or dominating power resided there while innovation and thought was the preserve of the city. In the modern age this power gap has decreased, but cities still found themselves constrained by the legacy power of the hinterlands in the institutions of the state. This can vividly be seen in the structure of the American Congress and Electoral College. When those institutions were established a significant power imbalance between rural and urban populations existed in the favor of the rural population, but this has now been much reduced, although many institutions do not yet reflect it.

In the more optimistic and utopian 1950s and 1960s, Constantinos Doxiadis developed and promoted the concept of 'existics' which imagined human settlement formed by an integrated worldwide surface of individual blocks whose wise planning and management was the key urban professional challenge. That human settlement was to be an enlightened, middle class, public and socialist world such as the one some science fiction writers describe. However, those rose-colored glasses were exchanged for a darker view of urbanization from the 1970s onward. Students of urban affairs began to know this urbanization in a more negative light as a source of social anomie, pollution, congestion and massive slum settlement. This encouraged efforts to explore the potential for rural and secondary towns growth pole development to actually reduce urbanization.

Sometime around the turn of the 21st Century in response to the development of Millennium Development Goals a new avenue of discussion opened up for urban affairs - that of urban growth for economic well-being. Suddenly cities, and mega-cities were our friends even though the vast majority of their populations would not be the utopian middle class, but a global working class linked to the global business and planning establishment. At the same time rural areas and smaller urban settlements were seen as unsustainable and backward - except for large investors and managers. Now we could look forward to global urban networks free of their retrograde hinterlands and moving into the brave new work of high technology which would need a global management structure and massive funding. Unlike the utopias of earlier visionaries, this new world would be a utopia without the utopians. This millennial metropolis would be a private utopia for the new techno-managerial elite.

Before Brexit and the election of Donald Trump, there seemed to be an unstoppable lobby for addressing climate change and promotion of carbon credit programs, and an explosion of interest in and boosterism for the urban sector with regard to resiliency and economic growth. In addition there was a rapid proliferation of urban-oriented web content and pseudo-organizations, and domestic and global urban networking and policy advocacy activity became an interest for large funding organizations, although urbanization had already been an increasingly important trend of human settlement in the Post-Colonial Era.

Then, suddenly *after* Brexit and the election of Donald Trump the scene changed dramatically. Now there are firmly two schools of thought concerning the massive urbanization underway around the world, connected with two different outcome interests. One of these sees the great potential of the urban explosion for economic growth and prosperity, and the other for endless traffic jams and commutes, massive slums, unaffordable housing and services, and unmanageable environmental pressures. Both of these schools wish to be considered futurists of a sort. One is utopian and the other dystopian.

One of these schools, represented by Bloomberg and other globalists, promotes cities as independent entities networked around the world and dominating their hinterlands as the queen bee dominates her drones. Many observers and pundits began to note with excitement that world cities are the engines of the information economy and that the information economy is the modern economy. Many, like Richard Florida, also noted with delight how these cities are also the home of the knowledge class and the social vanguard of a new global society.

However, no honest assessment of contemporary urban political economy was attached to that world view. Obsession with large scale urbanization, efficiency, unlimited growth and mobility - rather than quality of life - as a sine qua non of wellbeing - was unquestioned. Movement from one social contract to another in the case of population leaving older areas for newer ones, leaving rural for urban areas, and leaving less developed for developed countries was assumed to be cost-neutral - or at least to have no cost to the techno-managerial elite as they removed themselves from the realities of everyday plebian life as discussed in previous chapters.

There has not been much discussion about the implications of urban-rural and power city-subservient city divergence on the nation state. Historically metros and capital cities were the pinnacle of national identity and culture, albeit with a subculture of diversity. With London voting in great opposition to the British hinterland in the Brexit Referendum and a similar trend in the 2016 US Presidential Election, we can see a conflicted future where metros are detached from their hinterlands and long to unite with their sister metros around the world.

The recent urban exuberance has been followed by the suggestion that power cities should become politically independent from their hinterlands and even from the nation states to which they belong in order to form independent associations with other power cities. There have even been some, like Richard Florida, who went so far as to suggest that the power cities with substantial creative classes take up an aggressive independence struggle against less progressive urban and rural areas. At the same time, the reality of the winner take all global economy has meant that not all cities have this exalted status. In fact, the heart of the issue is confined to a very limited number of power cities within a very long list of world cities.

There is no ignoring the fact of massive urbanization. It is also obvious that many cities are becoming estranged from their hinterlands. A few cities are prospering greatly from their own predominance and from the emerging hierarchical structure of innumerable cities around the world that serve as warehouses and incubators of labor for and consumers of modern living. This overall urban system is remarkably precarious and is one of the wonders of the modern world. It depends on energy, automation and mobility, not on ideas or the creative class directly. The vast majority of input needed to provide energy, automation and mobility comes from 'deplorables' who are not part of the creative class or residents of the crystal cities. The labor needed for almost all components of modern life has been and continues to be greatly reduced as a result of increased production efficiencies and the impact of improved product design in delivery to the consumer. Of course, the cost of environmental impacts and waste production have not yet found their place in the financing and responsible management of the global urban system.

The New Gigantic Urban Scale

The globalist, neo-liberal agenda has suppressed the costs of massive world population growth by instead promoting the idea that population growth is needed for economic growth and that with urbanization and education the growth will slow. This is just an intellectual sleight of hand. World population is at the highest level in human history and its rate of growth, even if it slows, will never result in a reduced population under safe and peaceful conditions.

Even the scourge of HIV/AIDS has failed to significantly restrain the population growth in Africa.

At the same time as the existence and impact of the population explosion is minimized or dismissed, modern problems increasing in scale, severity and manageability are treated as unrelated or ignored. Such problems are governance, waste management, environmental degradation and pollution. Yet most of the problems are due to the increased urbanization and scale of population and activities. Since today's population levels are previously unknown in human history, there is little in our social memory that directly or effectively addresses these problems.

So the challenges are how to provide for, manage and occupy the new global urban populations. Taking the providing for as a first challenge, we can see that we are doing a remarkably good job at this. Urban areas only rarely face famine or resource shortages. In fact, the greatest problems that urban areas have faced until now have been war and civil disorder. But, just because we have managed to provide for urban populations in the past does not mean that we can continue to do so successfully and with assurance.

A possible energy-based collapse like the one environmental analyst, Nafeez Ahmed, has written about could come in three main forms: gradual, sudden or parabolic. Ahmad suggests that collapse has already started as a gradual process that might change into a parabolic one. Of course the increasing parabolic crisis could also change into a sudden collapse. In any event we should accept that there is a good chance that we are already entering the collapse, perhaps better termed crisis. Futurist euphoria over smart cities with new forms of technology assumes that technical possibility implies social manageability and financial affordability. Since smart cities are based on availability of high levels of energy supply and technical organization, there is no guarantee that smart cities will be less expensive or affordable even if they manage to be more efficient.

Even within the fortunate global knowledge power cities, only a small part of the population are among the creative class. The majority of the population even in the most advanced cities are worker bees who are insecure, mobile and detached from their hinterlands. This has resulted in a majority world population that has no geographic, national, social or economic power - at this time. Future predictions suggest that production labor from most of this population will not be needed in the next several decades. Then only a small group will continue with creative concept development, and the natural resource extractors in the hinterland will continue their insecure and uncertain toil, but the urban worker bees will have no regular and essential work.

When that scenario becomes a reality universal basic income, or universal basic services will be needed to satisfy and manage the remaining unneeded population. If this universal support is the same everywhere then there would be no incentive to relocate - but that could never be achieved. Instead, as we see today with massive migrant movements, the unneeded population will move to the most advantageous places, and place an increasing burden on those. This could eventually result in a limited number of power cities in addition to the hinterland and non-knowledge cities. It is far from certain whether the small knowledge class in the new power cities will be able to dominate their own worker bees as well as and the vast less-developed cities that are fast becoming an urban hinterland themselves.

Alternatives for Financing Global Urban Living

Most of the world is concentrating in larger urban areas where services are under-provided and backlogged, and where resources are limited and declining. Where will the resources for the global urban system come from when even basic services cannot currently be provided? The world has almost certainly receded from its affluence high water mark and now cannot hope to mobilize adequate resources from traditional factory-based consumer/worker synergies.

Whether planned or unplanned, there must eventually be location exit or entry taxes to capture the abandonment of social commitment, or to cover new unpaid access to existing investments. In the past countries such as south Africa, China and Russia have restricted rural to urban migration and China has never given up on this concept. Services are more extensive and expensive in urban areas but increasingly there is less and less work that pays enough to cover the cost of those services. In wealthier countries the concept of basic income is being discussed, a variant of which is a national shareholder system that provides shares in dynamic sectors of the economy to all citizens rather than only to the one per cent. If such a system is not introduced to discourage benefit migration there will be more such rural to urban movement bans and population control in the wider world as well.

Without a major intervention the current wealth inequality will continue and increase. Moreover, more and more of the world's population will have increased urban needs, but reduced employment and self-sufficiency. There is no peaceful alternative under those conditions, but to distribute the wealth and income under some form of universal basic income or universal basic services. However, there is a limit to this also, and it is really unlikely that enough wealthy individuals, countries and cities will be ready to share their bounty with the rest of the world. The nascent concept of universal basic income at present is still North American and Euro-Centric, assumes current socioeconomic conditions that are not shared with the rest of the world, and is far from assured public policy in any country. The most problematic assumptions behind universal basic income are those of family size, life expectancy worker-to-population ratio and structure of life activity without the necessity of having a job. Universal basic income is beyond the scope of simple planning and administration, and ultimately falls in the realm of political economy, where the practical limitations of resources will ultimately require the difficult clarifications of affordability, eligibility and enforceability.

If financial resources continue to be inadequate for urban services at the same time as increasingly desperate people flock to power cities, conditions will ultimately be ripe for civil unrest as a means to express dissatisfaction. Of course, at this time worker bees are still affluent enough to be pacified, but no future scenario predicts that can be maintained for long. This suggests that the developing police state structures around the world will be combined with smart city technology to prevent or delay urban civil unrest.

The world's power cities at various stages of development around the world cannot yet fully dominate their hinterlands, span the great distances between themselves, assuredly sustain all their internal middle and labor class populations, provide the new land use and living environment required for the creative and techno-managerial class and assert their political independence from nation states all at the same time. They will have to resolve several if not all of these challenges in order to achieve their hubristic dream. Can this be done and what are the steps that they urgently need to take? If they succeed or fail, what will be the impact on historical political, economic and administrative structures?

Chapter 7 - Historical Political Economy of Urban America

We have seen how within countries and worldwide, power cities are emerging to change human social and economic systems and to dominate them within their growing spheres of influence, both internal and external to the city, challenging traditional central place theory assumptions, and even having their own systems dominated by a limited number of more powerful power cities. Lesser cities, countries and the hinterlands are being manipulated and drained by power cities, but power cities themselves, while comparatively much better off, are themselves fragile in competition with the more powerful power cities, and even inside power cities themselves, a similar power stratification exists and is developing in new forms. The evolution of that stratification is the subject of this chapter.

One of the important structural changes in the political economy of the United States as it transitioned from a frontier to an industrial society was the shift in the balance of the population from small towns and rural areas to large urban areas. Even at the present time, American society is divided to a significant extent between the descendants of frontier settlers, descendants of industrial age immigrants. In <u>Trapped by History</u> I outlined the nature and progress of this division and the political economy effects on American society. These two population groups were not only divided by technology and sector of the economy, but also by historical influences, location, ethnic and cultural origin and social/political orientation. One of the most striking features of this division is that industrial age immigrants had very little opportunity to build capital while almost all frontier age settlers established private assets.

This situation was further reflected in different attitudes toward organized labor. Frontier age settlers had assets that allowed them to function and survive independently since they were self-producers or rented assets to others, so they opposed outside labor claims on their wealth. Industrial age immigrants in contrast were totally dependent on the owners of capital for daily survival and had extremely limited opportunities to build capital out of low current income. This explains their support for labor unions, their attraction to urban politics as a means of extracting wealth from owners of capital, and their generally aggressive, adversarial and opportunistic characteristics. The economic progress of industrial age immigrants as a whole was slow and ultimately constrained by the onset of the Great Depression. It was the Post-World War II era with the worldwide demand for reconstruction and American technology which provided a rocket launch for the industrial age immigrants that boosted them beyond even the prosperity of frontier age settlers - for a brief period of about 20 years - *but which seemed much longer and came to be expected as normal in the United States.*

The Post-World War II suburbanization subsidies, high wages and convenient long and short term financing structures made it possible for industrial era immigrants to buy houses and establish capital in them for the first time. For that group this was a great step, but that housing capital was not income earning, and maintaining ownership largely depended on continued industrial employment. Unfortunately for this group the Post-World War II boom did not last long enough for many of them to convert employment-linked home ownership into productive or transferable assets, as had been the case for descendants of frontier era settlers.

In fact, employment-linked *home ownership* had never been comparable to the *property ownership* of frontier era settlers because the property of descendants of frontier-era settlers was usually productive in some way and was often owned free and clear, with limited taxes rather than purchased through installments linked to industrial employment, and taxed at urban levels. Nevertheless, employment-linked home ownership was ultimately enough to provide the basis for the large labor class to consider itself part of the Great American Middle Class. In so thinking, the labor class considered those less fortunate to be of a different and competing class, although they themselves had been in much the same position decades earlier. Then suddenly beginning even in the mid-1960s the economy began to change, and sector by sector the labor component of the Great American Middle Class began to drop out of that class by losing industrial-era income, but also by losing home value and ownership.

Since this process was gradual and not across all industrial sectors at once, the impact was somewhat muted, especially since there was sustained and increasing affluence in other sectors and regions. Of course the frontier-era descendants for a time managed to straddle the old and emerging new economies with the aid of cheap imported consumer goods, rising demand from massive new immigration and the use of historical assets to subsidize education. It should be noted that consumer goods that once had nearly asset value, now had become short term disposable consumables, representing a stealth loss of wealth to global business and less-developed countries.

At the same time, for many people this was a consumption boom-let or even boom time, although for most it involved a drawdown in assets, and increased labor input in hours and number of family members working. Since employment was increasingly focused on urban centers there was a substantial movement from small towns and rural areas to medium and large urban areas, although not to the central business districts. Then in a very brief period these trends accelerated and left large areas of the country, sectors of the economy, smaller urban and rural areas, and large sections of the population impoverished and disenfranchised. Since mass industrial-era wages were a thing of the past, two-income and childless families nearly maximized, and non-wage dependent household assets were greatly reduced, in-demand portable skills and ability to locate in the new power cities were the only means of prospering.

In addition to the two classes of frontier settler and industrial-era immigrant descendents, a new class has emerged which has yet to be properly analyzed. That class is the "new immigrants." The new immigrant class is largely an urban class. Often this class is more risk-tolerant than the other classes and has been able to gain significantly from increasing power city power and wealth. Immigration today has a much lower practical cost than in previous generations, and much greater benefits. Moreover, since economic growth is concentrated in urban areas, and the new immigrants have continued linkages with home countries, limited allegiance to place and general commons community, more inclination to leverage family labor, ethnic contacts and shared assets, discomfort with taxes and regulations, and often preferential educational and employment opportunities, the new immigrants have raised the intensity and cost of living in power cities to the detriment of the majority of native-born Americans of all ancestry.

Since this demographic change occurred at a time of high social amenity expectation, and in the absence of industrial-era wealth and widespread individual income-producing assets, local governments have faced increasing difficulties in raising revenues. Local governments have used many financial techniques to manage their budget demands, but ultimately the limitations of tax revenues from the Great American Middle Class have became painfully apparent, leaving only the most affluent persons, businesses and institutions, and future expectation of increased population or revenues through bond-financing with significant capacity to financially support urban society.

The affluent persons, businesses and institutions are increasingly alienated from local societies and now want their wealth to be used for their own interests rather than those of the general community.

Moreover, their financial resources are increasingly relocated and concentrated in fewer and fewer power cities, rather than having a general spatial distribution. That means that at best there are few urban areas that can benefit directly from tapping these resources as can be seen in the intense and expensive current competition for a new Amazon headquarters - and that effective financial subsidies for non-power cities will have to come from the central government tax net.

Chapter 8 - The Great American Suburban Experiment

Particularly since the end of World War II the United States was the beneficiary of fortuitous and deceptive economic conditions that ironically discouraged stable communities and local control of assets. Suburbanization was one outcome of the deceptive Post-World War II American prosperity that was supported by government policies and the availability/affordability of low-cost petroleum products. Now that many Americans are beginning to see the actual weak/manipulated foundation of this prosperity, the role of a number of recent events and policies in bringing about a major social and political restructuring in America can be seen.

For example, huge investments had been made in industrial facilities, urban housing and equipment in the period after 1870 until around 1950. After 1950 much of this investment was lost due to the suburbanization promoted by developers, transportation improvement, government subsidies; and by relocation from undesirable urban social and financial conditions. This change was presented as modernization or improved efficiency from new development patterns and construction, but represented a huge financial, not to mention social loss, from the extensive abandonment of existing facilities.

Traditional industrial facilities and urban settlements were usually located where all sorts of urban services could be provided very efficiently. Late 19th and early 20th Century suburbanization to accommodate a growing population was largely self-financed by developers and other business interests (such as electricity companies) through fixed infrastructure such as streetcars, trams and other rail transport such as commuter rail which were oriented to the CBD. In contrast, Post-World War II suburbanization was promoted by the construction of new public-funded infrastructure (at a higher capacity due to maturing urban standards), provision of government subsidized mortgages, and the use of private cars and radial roads.

There was definitely a basic attraction to suburban living as part of the American frontier myth. In addition subsidized mortgages and road construction provided a wealth transfer from urban residents to suburban residents. Construction, furnishings, private recreational equipment, and car sales increased substantially to fill the new suburban living spaces. Along with developers and banks, rural and semi-rural land owners benefitted from massive land sales and development. Since so much more personal and transportation space was available in the suburbs consumption increased to a new level. However, sufficient public facilities did not exist in the suburbs so they had to be built new and quickly, adding initially unsubsidized costs to suburbanization. A good example of this is the use of mobile trailers for schools. Taxes were generally lower in suburban areas due to that very lack of facilities and new facilities may have been of a better standard than those that were there before. However, taxes on the original residents were increased considerably over a short time to support the higher level of services, and increased suburban demand improved economic opportunities there in the first stages of suburbanization.

The Character of Suburban Society

The new suburban residents were a composite of immigrant America but with generally less representation of some minorities. Although the earlier American urban experience had provided modern sector jobs in areas where the workers were drawn from different groups and physical communities, in most individual communities the residential settings provided common historical, economic, religious and ethnic group support. However, in the new suburbs residents had limited inherited common bonds. Suburban residents worked at different organizational levels, in different economic sectors and with different remuneration; came from different ethnic groups and sectarian associations, and had different historical and geographic experiences. As a result, the common bonds in the suburbs were the school, public services and taxes, the mass media and the consumption of goods and services.

The suburban experience reached its zenith with school age children. Television, radio, newspapers, magazines, comic books, books and markets (especially malls) became the common identity of suburban youth. Even though they might have ethnic or sectarian differences at home, the common experience was largely beyond those differences which only adjusted the common experience in minor ways for most youth. Examples of home differences would be religious days, holidays, some dietary restrictions, etc, which were largely surmounted by clever marketing and product design. The common youth experience was mostly independent of home culture. Powerful general external society influence on the primary home culture had been observed throughout America's history, but the suburban experience inserted daily culture as paramount and home culture as secondary. This was a major change. There were some differences that sprang from the home culture that persisted, but those differences were almost invisible within the daily shared culture.

Home differences were largely denied until specific stages of life when they produced some rifts in the suburban youth culture. Examples of these are ethnic group stages of life that ultimately bring children back to their own people and tradition anytime from puberty to college, marriage, children, retirement and death, but this was a declining force. An increasing new force was the choice by some to move away from the common suburb for college and career which often introduced socioeconomic changes which segregated the once common suburban - and also urban ethnic community - unity. However, as long as the economic engine of employment and consumerism remained strong, the majority of those who grew up in suburbs remained as an apparent community, and for almost three generations the economic engine was more or less strong enough to maintain this influence until new and even fundamentally conflicting cultural groups entered the suburbs.

On the surface this new cultural composition had little impact on the suburban community because of the common economic, media and consumption environment. However, these new cultural groups often sought to establish group unity in order to separate themselves from the larger suburban community for unique social as well as economic benefits, but remained within the broader economic circle. These efforts have not always been successful, but are widely practiced and range from physical neighborhood segregation to offering culture/religion/language classes, arranged marriages, and endogenous business relations.

However, as the ethnic composition of America has changed more and more suburban youth are experiencing dual identities in dual environments, often appearing to have no conflict within each. Ultimately, however, when the engine of employment and consumerism slows, the superficial shared culture will have very little strength and any remaining core cultures will emerge. The losers in that scenario will be those who have no core culture, or more clearly, those who have traded or converted their core culture for the shared media and consumption culture.

To the extent that America became suburbanized, the old unity of common family/ethnic experience and values became frayed. As a result, true ideology has declined, leaving only the general and subjective issues of economic opportunity and social equity for political debate. To the extent that unifying core ideological and cultural values have declined, political consensus has been a loser from the suburbanization process, since most family situations are now to some extent unique and share few interests directly with others - presenting a general fragmentation. Still, suburbanization has provided some physical community stability in that the new communities became older communities and many residents remained in place. However, in the more recent suburban generation, housing was often seen as part of savings, income and investment rather than as an identity and further weakened physical community identity.

Long Term Political and Economic Challenges of Suburbanization

It is well known that suburbanization and inter-regional migration have reduced the tax base in older built up urban areas and partially re-imposed those taxes in newly developed suburban areas. Even if this were a straight quid pro quo where tax and population changes were balanced it would still adversely affect the older urban areas, but no such balance was achieved in practice. Many more public institutions and services had previously been built up in older urban areas than would ever be replicated in suburban areas, so the loss of any tax base in older urban areas certainly caused local economic stress. Suburbanization and interregional migration (in effect, extra-suburbanization) resulted in a reduction of the middle class in most core urban areas. In areas where the rich still lived in the core areas they also moved out, except in some of the largest urban areas - which have now become power cities. Many of the original urban inhabitants and participants in long term urban public investments (not individually, but as a group) physically removed themselves from those areas and exited from an implied, but not binding contract to support those investments.

This trend was countered in a limited way by the so-called gentrification movement of Yuppie and bohemian young adults (who have morphed into today's creative and techno-managerial classes) into core urban areas. However, it is not at all clear if this will be a long term trend and whether it can compensate for or survive the financial crisis of core urban areas. In general the core urban areas reflected an increased proportion of the poor whose contributions were much less than the cost of legacy services they were offered. At the same time the more affluent began to prefer consumption of private rather than public recreation and education services, depriving the cities of at least their participation if not also their taxes. Cities countered the loss of tax base by taxing the businesses and affluent residents that still remained, but that was still not sufficient. Some cities tried to institute benefit taxes on commuters who lived in the suburbs, but worked in the core city. Other cities annexed suburban and exurban areas through various means.

Ultimately, none of these methods could replace a dynamic urban middle class, and cities have been temporarily saved by Federal subsidies and immigration. Most Federal subsidies are generally overlooked by the American public because they creep into the system without much direct impact or explanation. This was the case with Federal urban subsidies. Since core urban areas could not maintain their infrastructure and services and did not have the power to compel those who had left to pay to sustain them, Federal subsidies were developed for various urban sectors. The philosophical argument for imposing an exit tax or movement control on those who are part of a long term public investment when they leave a jurisdiction is an interesting one, but goes beyond the scope of this chapter.

The Federal Government stepped in to provide funding and promote immigration to replace the loss of middle class residents and sustain the built up urban infrastructure. If this had not happened the infrastructure and public services would have had to be substantially reduced causing great loss to the existing plant, social upheaval and regional dislocation. This would have been the natural course of things, but it was not allowed. The cost of sustaining the previous urban status quo was subsidized by the entire country, and to some extent by other countries, through the Federal budget and immigration. This state of affairs was not conceptually satisfactory to the majority of residents in cities, suburbs or exurbs, but it was an excellent short/medium term bridge solution and benefited the power elite and their techno-managerial agents.

As time marched on the costs continued to rise with no sustainable alternative to declining taxes. During some of this period the large Federal subsidies/bailouts allowed municipal service standards to be maintained and sometimes even raised as a result of temporary economic bubble prosperity, immigration and unsustainable municipal bond borrowing. Even the greatly helpful immigration began to shift to suburban and less urbanized areas. Justification for municipal bond funding was often misrepresented by intellectual sleight-of-hand arguments to address needs of urban decline, when its proper use is for managing long term urban growth.

At the same time that all the mechanisms for covering urban service costs had been exhausted, the bubble international reserve currency economy and Federal financial resources began to decline. This allowed the cumulative effect of American suburbanization to be felt in direct terms. Cities such as Detroit would have to reduce even their basic services and physically remove some infrastructure plant. Yet, those cities and the entire United States tax base had been unnaturally sustaining them since at least the mid-1960s. A large part of the capital investment and maintenance expenditure spent in those cities since the 1960s would now be lost.

The great railroad legacy of the United States was rapidly abandoned in the Post-World War II period in favor of road transport for both goods and passenger movement. Just as suburbanization gave more locational and lifestyle choices, the use of trucks for goods transport allowed the expanded choices for manufacturing and commercial facility location. Because the national road system was subsidized, and the abandonment or inefficient use of rail facilities required no exit charge, considerable national wealth was also lost in this transition. This change greatly reduced the utilization of physical plant tied to railway lines, and could only be afforded through subsidies, and the suburbanization and regional migration process. It was also supported through low petroleum and non-core land prices. Ultimately the loss of physical plant and efficient transportation was not the full loss. The subsidy of consumption (volume) instead of production (value) resulted in the expenditure of a large part of national income on extensive and less durable imported products that ultimately would have no value, and required unproductive time in their use as well as costly storage space.

In the 1960s the economic benefits of suburbanization were realized by many people at different levels - from individual homeowners building their own structures on their own land to small developers who prepared land for development, to builders who put their money up front for construction in anticipation of home buyers, to large turn-key subdivision developers. The movement away from the core cities also allowed small business to take advantage of new opportunities in decentralized locations. The suburbanized environment created a boom similar in scale to that of the late 19th and early 20th Century explosion of large urban areas, the Gold Rush or the later Alaska Pipeline bonanza - but for a much larger population all over the country. Unlike that earlier robber baron environment, the suburban boom had very low scales of economic operation and was much more egalitarian. That encouraged many Americans to think that the United States was truly the land of opportunity again, and that the country belonged to them. At least it seemed that way, and the new situation kept many Americans so occupied that they could not see what was being done in the smoke-filled rooms of technocrats and the real decision makers.

Just as in earlier booms, there was no structure in place to manage or control the broader impact this time of suburbanization. The United

States could only ride the wave and try to stay afloat. This was a huge challenge for most communities and institutions since they had little experience in dealing with this type of rapid growth and community change. Moreover, the benefits of suburbanization to the Great American Middle Class in that period have ultimately been out-weighed by the comparative losses from power city dominance.

Tremendous demands were suddenly and continuously being placed on suburban communities; and new personalities and social behavior were introduced into previously static systems. New residents found the system poorly responsive and entered community politics. At first the existing power structures prevailed, but after the first wave of development profits and with significant population and social changes, the historical power structures became undone. In my own home town of Raleigh, North Carolina this could be seen over 40-50 years as a politically and socially conservative urban society changed into a liberal enclave in a conservative state. The means used to bring about this change was the settlement of an increased and diverse population, much the same way as it was used in the Soviet Union, China and Afghanistan to control various parts of their regions.

As a result suburban and new growth area institutions became less oriented to the historical and local community and more linked with the national techno-managerial system. This resulted in a homogeneity of operations, and ultimately a homogeneity of management, professional and political-economy philosophy across the country; so much so that managers were chosen with respect to credentials and not with respect to their residence, position in the community or moral stature. This was a marked change from the 1960s when some university tenure committees even evaluated candidates with respect to morals as well as academic credentials. The Civil Rights Act, and subsequent rules and legislation covered employment and participation in all but the most restrictive private activities so that traditional or local values could no longer be enforced in local institutions – institutions which were established to serve the local community! We should consider whether this is different in substance from the Soviet commissar or colonial systems.

As a long term result of suburbanization American common public culture became dislocated from place and history, and transformed into a superficial and transitory experience. The residual culture was that of the individual sometimes at the individual household level, which was no longer part of a social contract. Vast physical plant investment was lost. Newly developed areas did not have the same density so services were fewer and more expensive. Federal or national funding for declining urban areas replaced local funding lost by migration and suburbanization, but the cost structures of core urban areas could not be reduced, so that net national benefits from suburbanization may have been negative, but this was concealed by Federal funding, immigration and debt financing. National subsidies were hidden as part of low transportation and oil prices, world reserve currency benefits, and indirect borrowing. Immigration and gentrification provided a generational distortion to this broader pattern. Political and social cohesion of suburban America was ultimately a chimera and could only be possibly replicated by emerging Internet-based virtual communities.

America is no longer the wealthy middle class country it was. From economic, social and political perspectives it can no longer afford the suburban development paradigm and its society. That doesn't mean that the suburban experience should be condemned, because it was a pleasant experience for many people over a long period. America just has to move on. The important task now is to identify the new urban structure that can honestly afford basic urban services, and to try to minimize the losses that result from transitioning away from the old suburban world.

This monumental endeavor will be at the scale of the Great Depression-era programs, and of wartime resource mobilization. Contrary to the ideas of many urbanists and futurists, this cannot be a globalist venture, but must be a society and nation building program guided by the public sector. Although there can and must be private sector involvement, such an ambitious undertaking must have a commons-oriented vision and be supported by changes in the political economy such as universal basic income or universal basic services. Unlike the utopian and futurist ambitions of the past, basic urban services are no longer supported by economic and demographic growth, or by the wealth and social unity that were present in earlier times. This time a new paradigm based on post-industrial conditions has to be established for a new 'city on a hill'.

Chapter 9 - Elite Segregation and The Collapse of the American Social Contract

Unlike in earlier times when few social amenities were required and limited charitable funds could have major impact in social uplift, *now the vast majority of urban society requires a subsidy for all necessary social amenities*. Unfortunately, now the urban population no longer has any strong ethnic, employment, community, religious or cultural linkages to the philanthropic class, and the philanthropic class has increasingly diverted its wealth to charitable contributions away from local communities for selfish ideological interests - and to other parts of the world.

The new power and techno-managerial elite classes now want to control their charity and subsidies for visibility and high impact, and do not want to provide mundane and un-remarkable local government operating support. Instead, they even want to satisfy their special preferences separately from the standard urban public services offered to their fellow citizens. That has resulted in a number of disturbing new trends which threaten the sustainability of urban systems as well as the broader social unity. The most egregious examples of these are the loss of support for broad-based public schools in favor of private and class-oriented schools, gated communities, privately owned public spaces with private security, etc. These developments lead to segregation of once-common public spaces into those for the less fortunate and those for them who can afford customized and controlled services. When that rupture takes place the public spirit needed for financially and operationally supporting common services starts down a slippery slope that ends in a fractured society.

At the broader level the power elite have developed even more disturbing dystopian ideas such as that of the Seasteading Institute which envisions boats or floating developments in ocean space, Elon Musk's Mars colonialization ambition, Chinese proposals to construct islands in the sea near Colombo, Sri Lanka, other investor plans to construct islands in the sea near Jakarta, Indonesia, and the recent Saudi Arabian dream to develop a new age city, NEOM, independent of most of the Kingdom's normal administrative constraints.

This is related to a much broader effort at alienating land held under traditional and customary ownership in many countries in the world (such as Afghanistan where any land not held with a formal certified title can be claimed as the King's land and diverted to private use), and recent court rulings in the United States where eminent domain has been used to facilitate private development broadly defined as supporting a greatly stretched public interest.

The final result of all these trends is a dystopian society at international, national, regional and local levels where the power elite, the techno-managerial class, productive assets and revenue are socially, physically, administratively and legally separated from the mass of the population - including the former Great American Middle Class - even in the dominating power cities.

When the social contract at the national level breaks down, public amenities and quality of life usually become differentiated by location according to wealth. Today we are seeing such differentiation and the resultant stresses between regions which places national integrity in danger. We have not seen similarly clear stresses at the local level yet largely because of the state and national cross-subsidies that still enable basic services to function - and wealth stratification is still largely by jurisdiction rather than by service level *within* jurisdiction. The inevitable result of unrestricted markets controlled by a few and other current negative trends will be the complete functional separation of the power elite from the masses with respect to urban services even within the same jurisdiction. This is much more serious than physical segregation because it creates the conditions for proximate conflict.

Several years ago Murray Bookchin raised the issue of whether modern urban areas still allow for the formation and function of civic communities - even before the disturbing developments mentioned in this chapter became obvious. Today, segregation of the power and techno-managerial elite is well on its way toward creating an urban and global environment where civic communities no longer exist and cannot be recreated naturally or peacefully. The only hope of changing this course of social conflict is to re-integrate the power elite, the techno-managerial elite and the knowledge class with the broader society economically, socially and politically.

Chapter 10 - Evolution of Modern Urban Services and Finance

Administration and management of urban areas has been more or less undergoing changes since antiquity. Most importantly for our consideration in this book are the introduction of mass modern urban services as the result of a successful industrial era, and the challenges of the current post-industrial era.

Until the advent of modern urban systems, cities large or small, generally provided limited and low quality services. The industrial era in developed countries generally provided the urban capital needed to fund the development of at least adequate core infrastructure systems by the public or private sectors. In factory towns, labor housing, industrial plant and all basic infrastructure was provided directly by the private sector. However, it seems that urban capital generation began to decline as the industrial era came to an end and did not continue into the post-industrial era, or at least its purchasing power no longer allowed development of major core infrastructure systems that served all classes. Since urban infrastructure systems were already in place and had service life measured in decades, the decline in industrial era wealth was not felt in decreased services for some time - although deterioration in private building stock was painfully obvious. At some point in the middle of the 20th Century funding of operations and maintenance (O&M) declined, but urban systems could largely withstand this because neglected O&M does not have an immediate impact on most infrastructure, but is only felt when cumulative deterioration causes systems to actually break down.

Early infrastructure systems reflected a mix of public and private investment, but over time political/social pressures resulted in most systems being owned by or seriously regulated by government. This inevitably resulted in inadequate maintenance and failing services. In any event, after decades of use core infrastructure needs upgrading or replacement. That requires even more than the original level of industrial era investment, because land, labor, materials, and socio-environmental costs become more expensive over time. When this situation begins to demand urgent attention, the costs are usually more than city governments are able to meet, sometimes resulting in retrenchment as has been experienced in Detroit and some mid-western states in recent years. As a result, city governments turn to long term borrowing through the sale of bonds, state or Federal government grants (with no accompanying support for long term O&M), and the private sector as in much earlier times, although now this is often euphemistically called public-private partnership (PPP).

All of these infrastructure financing mechanisms assume and depend on the future good health of the overall urban economy, which is not assured in every case. Even under the best of circumstances, it is only the wealthiest and newly developing cities that can provide or secure adequate capital and O&M needed for city-level trunk public infrastructure. In the case of wealthy cities this means higher taxes or higher user charges, widening the divide between power cities and the rest, as well as increasing the de facto entrance fee to those aspiring to reside there.

In suburban and sunbelt areas where new trunk infrastructure was built over decades and the density of users was much lower than in older cities, new in-fill and densified development is placing increased demand for services that was not anticipated earlier. The main reason that these areas could afford core infrastructure at the same time as it became difficult for industrial-era cities is that costs, scale and dependent population there were lower, but the scale of these factors are now catching up with those of the older industrial-era cities. Where cities and urban areas are not wealthy enough to support core infrastructure for new satellite towns, distant suburbs or even affluent areas within the city boundaries, infrastructure to these areas may ultimately have to be provided through a decentralized structure without common standards. While this may sound heretical to some urban professionals, it is already being practiced for some services in privately-owned public spaces (POPS) and in gated communities.

As the world population increases and becomes more urbanized, the cost of basic services such as transportation, clean water and waste management increases. There are no meaningful scale economies in this urban growth particularly because of the exponential nature of urban area growth. In contrast, rural areas and semi-urban areas do not need basic services because there are only individual needs and there is direct access to the necessary resources. In a rural areas, as long as density is not too high, employment is near to residence, food and natural resources are available from the local area, waste products are natural and can decompose in the environment, the amount of energy needed to support daily human activities matches that available from human labor, simple tools and machinery. That human living environment is a package of resources which humans need to access by their own skills.

The modern urban environment can be of two main types: historical settlement and new settlement. Of course some new settlements may be close to the same locations as historical settlements. The core issue of urbanization today is in fact the political economy in relation to settlements of these two types. Current urbanization is fundamentally different from all urbanization that has come before since it currently involves the majority, and will ultimately involve almost all, of the world's population.

Historical urban settlements were fundamentally different from rural settlements because of the social and technical organization that they developed. At the lowest level of development historical settlements straddled both urban and rural functions. This is noteworthy in waste disposal and water supply which remained as rural functions. However, as historical cities expanded, the exponential growth in occupied area meant that rural space and resources were not available nearby and ultimately that even locations within the city itself were at an inconvenient distance from each other. The result of this was the need to create internal systems for water supply, waste disposal and movement within the city, and even coordinated transport and markets for goods and materials imported from rural areas. Even until recent times in many historical cities internal systems were poorly developed or not developed, but the technical and medical knowledge of the modern era eventually forced most cities of the developed world and some colonial cities to implement basic waste management and water provision, and more recently markets and transportation facilities.

Mass transportation only became an issue in the modern era when technology began to separate urban work and residence. As mass transportation and public security developed both job and residence were freed from some of the constraints of the historical city, but geography, technology and cost continued to discourage most location changes. It was initially street cars and later the private motor vehicles that extended urban areas into less dense suburbs for the upper and middle classes. This was especially prominent in the United States where geography and general wealth did not restrict urban expansion. New development outside of the dense urban core allowed urban service provision to return to a more rural technology.

As urban areas grew outward new suburban areas were established within the area of influence of historical cities, but without connection to the core area urban services. The overall urban and metropolitan area densities decreased and not all land was developed, leaving Swiss cheese like gaps within urban areas. Development away from dense urban cores resulted in significant relocation, disinvestment and abandonment of many areas, and the removal of tax resources from the core area to the suburbs. This was an odd situation since many long term infrastructure investments had been made to cater for the peak work day use of urban services in the core area, while the new development pattern shifted much of the off-peak residential services use as well as a large part of the overall tax revenues to the new disbursed and fragmented suburbs, weakening the financial capacity of core areas to provide services. Later this was further complicated by regional and national rather than nearby suburban relocations.

Such was the pattern in the United States for several decades and slowly this pattern could even be observed to a lesser extent in other developed and even less developed countries. As more and more of the population have been brought into the urban economy, a greater volume of services must be provided at an urban standard because regulation has tightened to restrict any but standard development and services. Probably standards are too high and applied too extensively, due to the current emphasis on professional and management credentialization. The result is that developed countries now have urban standards that are applied and supported by all metropolitan areas for most of the population, but with varying densities and gaps in development continuity. Current wisdom is that the spatial development gaps should be filled in with new development and the density of development increased.

However, the prototype metropolitan design recommended today is based on density concentrations at transit nodes, leaving unaddressed the inefficiencies of finance and efficiency for other urban services in broad metropolitan areas. Practically speaking, centralized modern standard urban services can only be provided affordably in the richest and uniformly developed urban areas, as a result of diseconomies of system scale, jurisdictional restrictions and limitations on revenue collection. In less developed countries metropolitan areas cannot provide centralized urban service standards. As a result smaller new urban units such as housing societies provide specific urban service standards for their residents, but historical common metropolitan services cannot achieve desired standards. The best examples of this are in public security, solid waste management and transportation, but examples can also be seen in water, sewerage treatment, etc.

The lack of unified jurisdictions in American metropolitan areas is likely to present problems similar to those in less developed countries as the extensive existing infrastructure ages and needs replacement. This will mean that different standards of services will be planned and provided for different areas, and that common core services will be reduced and become difficult to sustain, especially where jurisdictional disputes emerge such as with the Washington, DC Metrorail System. In suburbs, new local services had been developed to be later connected with the historical metropolitan infrastructure system, but this will be increasingly difficult to achieve. Historical urban areas may delink from outlying new areas and even experience varied standards of service provision within their own areas as a maintenance equilibrium is established. The fragmentation of urban development and society that this scenario presents is a serious concern for the future civil order.

Until recently physical earth features such as rock formations, undulating terrain, rivers, etc. had restricted urban development. This can be seen especially in picturesque old European cities. However, modern technology now allows almost any geographic feature to be leveled, and with the new ideas promoted by The Boring Company, undercut. That leaves water bodies and other public land as the only spaces which provide secure buffers from new development and offers potential for increased density of development, but does not necessarily make the new required infrastructure affordable.

Urban development and construction capacity is now virtually unlimited and accessible, but the associated urban service standards require a separate affordability in the form of jobs and income, which has become increasingly weak in the key middle income range. As capital seeks out fewer and fewer opportunities for investment, urban development has emerged as a vast and popular option around the world due to growth. However, this investment has been focused on separate individual developments with the assumption of common urban standard infrastructure, but which cannot be sustained. It is likely that urban settlement and economic form, and service provision standards will have to be re-oriented soon and may cause many recent investments to fail.

The cost of urban infrastructure had been covered by the ultimately declining industrial capital. *However, the massive industrial era urban capital such as was generated in developed countries is a thing of the past (with the apparent exception of China). As a result, social welfare taxation is generally required to fund even existing basic urban infrastructure.* New infrastructure, even in the limited number of power cities, requires bond and private financing, with confident and attractive returns.

In less developed countries historical and economic conditions resulted in three types of city: the administrative city, the natural resource/trading city and the business city. There were variations on these three, such as low to moderate level infrastructure/industrial cities and the exceptional capital cities. These cities or towns represented a small proportion of the national populations, and provided basic infrastructure to a limited part of their urban areas and populations. In the post-colonial era all of these urban areas have grown, but industrial capital has generally declined and been transferred to export processing zones (EPZ) and other industrial areas outside of the city where housing for labor is not provided. This creates a form of decentralized infrastructure, where an adequate standard can be provided for a limited area without requiring a related cross-subsidy for the same level of services at the city level. However, this shifts a large public infrastructure burden onto the public jurisdictions where labor is housed, yet which lack access to industrial capital.

Today, the growth of urban areas in less developed countries is unprecedented, yet little of the growth is related to industrial employment. Since there is limited industrial capital, the vast majority of the population does not pay sufficient taxes to fund basic infrastructure, and financial capital does not have adequate capacity and security to fund basic infrastructure, the main source of urban infrastructure finance is government administrative revenue. This revenue comes from various taxes, duties, charges, etc., but has not been sufficient or dependable enough to cover the upkeep of the power city administrative class in addition to maintaining and providing existing services, let alone to support installment financing of new infrastructure. As a result, an increasingly urbanized developing world does not generate adequate wealth to support traditional city-wide urban infrastructure, the standard for which was based on a smaller urban scale and population, and greater capital wealth. In light of this challenging environment, provision of decentralized and cost-effective localized infrastructure with varying service levels, even in developed countries and particularly for non-power cities will increasingly be required.

In developed countries it appears that industrial capital has only been partially replaced for the time being by social welfare taxation or financial capital for urban infrastructure. At the same time financial capital has become more mobile and less dependable than industrial capital, and the share of labor in all capital has been steadily declining. These trends suggest that it will be difficult to finance initial basic infrastructure for complete urban areas even with long term local resource-backed financing, and that in the long term O&M would have to be financed by user charges in addition to general obligation funds. In this scenario, broad urban area infrastructure provision would be increasingly difficult as urban areas grow in size and population, with unregulated geographic dispersion and as capital from the industrial base declines.

Chapter 11 - Urban Service Provision Scenarios

Due to the current scale of population and the need to manage it in urban areas, basic service provision cannot be optional for local government in the post-industrial urban age, rather it is a necessity. As a result, political and administrative structures have generally allowed national governments to increasingly establish standards for services, but without ensuring combined funds for development and O&M of urban infrastructure. The conflict of mandated services with inadequate funding cannot continue in the modern urban age. There are four likely alternatives for urban service provision in the emerging urban world as given below.

1. modern urban world development is reversed by population reduction, reducing the demand for services
2. a two or three tier service level system is introduced that allows the most basic - but not the desired - services in urban infrastructure to be provided in all urban settlements, but allows higher standards of services to be isolated for the remaining middle class, and for the techno-managerial and power elite class
3. all citizens are allowed to choose where and how they live with no certainty or standard of municipal services, ultimately requiring local area and private arrangement of services - this would be the current conditions experienced in less developed countries combined with increased segregation of elites from the rest of the population
4. common services are provided as municipal monopolies for all of a single class of citizens only in approved and viable urban settlements where they are efficient and affordable, while guaranteed municipal services to other urban areas are phased out. We can call this scenario the Millennial Metropolis Model (MMM).

In the case of the first alternative, several questions are raised. In an urban world with service standards that cannot be achieved or afforded, the required social contract could provide for population control or reduction in exchange for those services. This raises a number of issues that are not attractive to many and this arrangement will not be voluntarily accepted by all citizens. Moreover, peaceful population reduction would take more than a generation and might not substantially reduce the per person cost.

The second alternative is already being implemented informally for the power elite and managerial class, but has not been understood or accepted by the rest of the population. Moreover, achievable basic service standards and provision have not yet been established with certainty. This would be an improvement of the current trend in that it would establish and provide standard services for all, but with different qualities.

The third alternative is in fact the default alternative which would provide for an unsustainable urban world that would be full of strife and conflict, and would create health and environmental impacts that could not be ameliorated. However, there would be a greater role for the private sector which might manage resources and systems better than the government sector could, but with great inequalities.

The fourth alternative could be seen by many people as the socialist alternative. This alternative would not allow enhanced services for any group and would limit freedom of location, but would provide standard services for all along with restrictive or coercive government measures.

Several important questions arise from this analysis: how would the four alternatives be managed and financed; how would administrative boundaries be drawn according to the urban service provision alternative implemented; what level of services would be provided for the remaining non-urban residents; and how will global migration be managed in the face of substantial variations among world city conditions and alternatives.

A challenge for all four alternatives is the inadequacy of a voluntary and broad social contract needed to implement them. All four will require some degree of coercion if the public has full knowledge of the conditions. Alternatives one, two and three could be implemented by either a people's government or the power elite with their techno-managerial class, or a combination of both. Alternative four could only be implemented by a people's government, because it would start the process to rectify the most egregious aspects of the current disparity between the power elite and the mass population.

Under all four scenarios national governments will be required to provide subsidies for urban services in line with the national tax/revenue resource distribution paradigm. This revenue sharing cannot be a capricious gifting of funds by the national government, but must be based on a consensus among national and local governments and established as a right and as a routine practice, which will require a deep analysis of costs and revenues, establishment of basic urban standards and a thorough public administration analysis.

None of the four alternatives presented above are fully satisfying in terms of the current Western understanding of political economy norms. However, it is the opinion of the author that there are no other alternatives, and that one of the four would prevail in each major urban area and its associated nation-state, even though each of the alternatives would involve substantial compromises.

For the purpose of this book, it is the fourth alternative, the MMM, that will be explored in the context of changing technology and a changing political economy.

Chapter 12 - The Millennial Metropolis Model - Universal Basic Services for the New Age

There is no greater urban visionary and futurist than le Corbusier. Self-appointed experts of the community development school have trashed le Corbusier by associating his concepts with terms such as brutalism and even fascism. Le Corbusier and other visionaries of the modernist period even as recent as Isaac Asimov placed great faith in systematic planning and organization. Everything had a place and the enemy was disorganization or anarchy. All this could work in theory and in the world of the future where everyone recognized order as protection from fear and want. In most science fiction writing this was the shape of the world of the future - but usually there was some deep doubt about the ultimate management or intention of the system.

The urban world of the future was almost always a socialist world where basic needs were met and most people were more or less equal. Most people also had basic education, functional skills, a civic sense and were law abiding so that ideas such as Isaac Asimov's moving sidewalks could be possible without concern for vandalism. Only the basic and society-level security precautions if any were needed. Overall it was a socialist vision of a middle class world. All the basic needs and systems were planned and organized by unknown persons somewhere. Mundane concerns had been eliminated and only structured work and recreation remained - like in Star Trek - but normally without the alien surprises.

That urban world of the future was almost always homogeneous and sometimes had some human variety, but the unifying bond was performance of one's job in the established system, if not with joy at least without resentment. Work was the purpose of life and there was rarely any unstructured aimless personal recreation. This was a world where some form of a universal basic services program was in use. Most basic services and functions were freely provided and only special personal preferences needed payment in credits. The urban world of the future was almost always high tech, but it also had a social contract.

As we start to conceive of a world with universal basic services we should first think of the things that are basic to living. If we live in the utopian urban world of the future there would be less personalization of residence and place of work. That means standardized use of electricity, communications, etc. Maybe we should consider providing these basic needs as a public service. We should ask whether anyone in our society can be expected to function without power and communications. If these are indeed necessities then why not provide these as a basic service package?

Of course, there are many items that straddle the need and desire divide such as food and medical care. Since those involve great current dispute, I prefer to skip them in this book. However, one other certain basic need is mobility. The concept of mobility is changing from that of specific individual movements and vehicles on corridors to one of coordinated movement on spider web-like facilities with universal accessibility. In the earlier-time utopian urban future the ideal transportation system would have been provided by coordinated network mass transit services linking limited efficient residence and work locations and travel times. However, today's disbursed urban development has resulted in limited coordination of extensive movements and limited use of network mass transit services.

To efficiently cater to the reality of the disbursed urban environment, customized mobility operations in the form of continuously circulating and hailable Uber- and Lyft-type transport services are needed. Since in theory this would reduce the need for private vehicles lying idle, considerable parking and circulation space would be freed up, and personal assets could be diverted away from motor vehicles since the cost of travel for an individual trip could be mainly based on as-needed and partial use of continuously operating vehicles. In this scenario a fleet of vehicles with drivers, or self-driving vehicles could have a fixed system cost and as a mobility service could also be provided as part of a basic services program. This could have an overall lower total social cost than the current payment system for as-used and less-responsive transit systems with restrictive area coverage. Those who wish to live in unique environments with larger residences and personalized transport would fall outside of this basic mobility service environment, but the convenience, efficiency and ubiquity of the new mobility services would be attractive to the majority of the public.

However, most urbanizing societies with dramatic population growth and heterogeneous populations are far from utopias with the strong social contracts and stable environments needed for making a governance change of this magnitude. In addition, the world population is in motion seeking the greatest benefits at the lowest cost. Success of providing basic services and mobility will depend on the re-establishment of a social contract for a world much more chaotic and heterogeneous than the utopias visionaries like le Corbusier expected.

Of course this new urban service provision system could not happen overnight since it requires a substantial change in the current social, economic and political governance underpinning. It is with a combination of basic services and urban planning for millennials that the process would most likely start with incentives to locate in areas with shared services and facilities planned to reduce travel, especially travel from home to work. In addition to similarities with medieval cities, this possible approach would also include elements of utopian community and factory town political economy structure. The most likely system to initially evolve in the millennial metropolis is one of vouchers sufficient to obtain a basic urban livelihood.

A basic urban livelihood would include a safe comfortable housing unit that has basic living, cooking, eating and sleeping space for an individual or a family, accounting for personal privacy preferences. We have had something like this in developed countries, but it was a welfare program rather than part of an improved political economy. Housing unit prototypes are already emerging in the private sector in urban areas such as New York and London where small affordable private living spaces are provided in buildings in convenient core areas. These are a good start, but do not address the broader political economy issues such as secure affordability, local shared facilities and proximity to work.

As an example we can imagine a realistic example of a typical millennial college graduate that cannot find a permanent career track job and has to work in the gig economy. Imagine that he does not wish to live in his parents basement, but wants some independence and interaction with others that might improve his overall well-being and opportunities. Housing with increased privacy and independence in comparison to college dormitory conditions would be very helpful for him, but to find an affordable unit in a safe serviced building and neighborhood, and to ensure the income to pay for it would be daunting. Moreover, since housing is not coordinated with nearby employment and social interaction/networking, there are additional costs for transportation and market-access.

With the growth of the gig economy, more and more people need to work in their own privately-provided spaces. Such spaces are often found inside residences, and in commercial/public spaces such as coffee shops, but these are neither socially desirable nor without cost. Shared work, learning, social and enterprise center spaces would be more efficient and socially beneficial as long as behavior codes are enforced. If adaptable shared work and social spaces are matched with nearby housing, mobility and social networking, private space needs can be greatly reduced. Since these facilities are required for large numbers of people it should not be difficult to imagine that they could be provided as part of a basic services system that would allow use of vouchers to access such residence/work neighborhoods in any suitable available location.

In addition to this basic living environment, other basic services such as water, electricity, sanitation, mobility and Internet, which are requirements for modern urban living, would also be provided as part of the basic services program. Basic clothing and food could be covered with specific vouchers. Primary and secondary education, childcare and routine medical services could also be provided to residents at the neighborhood level. Post-secondary education is expected to quickly re-orient to distance learning and not require significant cost beyond Internet access and shared learning spaces. All basic services should be within 1/4 - 1/2 mile of residential centers with the possible exception of traditional educational and major medical facilities. What would not be covered as part of basic services would be individualized fashion, entertainment, possessions, travel and interests and major medical expenses. If residents are able to earn income they would be able to use this as they wish, although there would also be less pressure to consume as a result of the changed living environment.

Key impediments to feasible and functional urban development have been the reliance on market forces and inadequate public consensus. This could be addressed by trial implementation of a basic services program which would make it possible to effectively plan for and provide efficient urban living environments. Increasing financial and lifestyle security would allow the reduction of private ownership of most items to provide greater efficiency in space utilization. Many items such as vehicles are not used most of the time and could be shared, reducing the space needed to park and store them. By reducing this need for space a greater density would be obtained allowing easier walking access to routine facilities, and greater social interaction would result with associated synergies. Visionaries such as le Corbusier and Doxiadis imagined similar shared urban spaces, but which did not provide the scale of localized work opportunities and reduced travel that are becoming more realistic in the new economy.

Personal space and travel would be reduced, reducing the common social cost burden. Individuals would have security to live and use public spaces regardless of whether they get paid - or get paid enough. Social isolation would be reduced and even anti-social behavior would be reduced because of many shared facilities and activities - there are probably not many mass murderers in college dorms. Of course, some people might be lazy and not work because they don't have to, but that could also happen if there were no basic services.

This environment may not be everyone's cup of tea, and other options could be provided in other locations. However, this structure could well serve a large and growing part of the population. There will be many who will have a strong negative reaction to this approach from the market and political perspectives. Ultimately the main challenge to implementing this type of urban political economy comes from the need to redistribute economic resources. That is a separate and lengthy subject. For the purpose of this book, it is not addressed in detail in order to focus on exploring the potential for improved urban efficiency.

If a discussion of economic resource distribution can be avoided for the time being, the next issues to be explored are those of individual behavior and preferences. Some would say that the basic services program will restrict individual preferences. To the contrary, individual preferences would not be restricted at all; only there would be fewer of them and if an individual wishes to choose a different living environment it would be possible if he earned the additional money to cover that. The real challenge for the United States and other societies is that of behavior control. In truth, many people choose to live in certain places mainly in order to avoid the behavior of other people. In order to organize and manage efficient and affordable urban living environments for large populations, some behaviors will have to be restricted such as loud music, privacy intrusion, uncivil behavior and intimidation. These are largely managed at college campuses so this should not present a major challenge. The urban basic services program would initially be voluntary, provide many benefits and only gradually cover large numbers of the population.

This program would begin with a number of nodal developments in central urban areas that can expand to be more or less contiguous with each other as in the Doxiadis Ekistics urban growth concept with shared large green/recreational spaces and regularly-spaced higher level service centers such as hospitals, colleges, and government. In developed countries this approach to urban development will reduce the demand for inefficient suburban development and new cities by facilitating densification of historical cities through efficient infill and redevelopment. This is not likely to be the case for urban areas in developing countries because of the lack of historical infrastructure. As a result, the greatest ideological challenge to implementing a basic services program in developed countries will come from the opposition to providing immigrants with this visible and measurable share of the national endowment.

The core emerging subject in the modern urbanizing world that needs to be addressed is that of the urban political economy. This is not the same as so-called urban economics. Urban economics supposedly deals with the use and price of land and resources in cities from a market perspective. With that as a reference urban planners seek to guide or allow investment where it is naturally inclined to go. In some cases incentives, penalties and regulations are used to improve urban system 'efficiencies' in light of the prevailing market forces. However, there are major constraints on this traditional, largely free-market approach. For example, people and businesses may wish to locate more efficiently, but regulations - and affordability - can prevent this. Facilitating such desired outcomes independent, or in spite of, market conditions is the domain of urban political economy.

As Post-World War II capitalism transitions into the new economy, it is becoming clearer day by day that consumption is or will soon be a greater human activity than work. Moreover, it is now clear that there is less productive work available than the labor seeking it, and that the share of labor in the economy is decreasing rapidly and that of capital is increasing. It is also clear that only a small portion of the population will be able to form the techno-managerial elite, and that the vast majority of the population will be more highly regulated with fewer job opportunities, higher costs and fewer resources.

Since it is increasingly difficult to generate assets from mere labor, demographic trends suggest that some form of wealth redistribution will be needed. If the structure of universal basic income is used, it would have to be aligned with the cost of urban residence and services. A weakness in this concept is the linkage to the market cost of urban residence and services, rather than to the services themselves. The use of universal urban basic services might be less ideologically attractive to many, but is potentially much more effective in addressing the wealth redistribution problem than universal basic income which would still have to respond to the privileged owners of capital who set the prices, profits and market supply.

Under an urban basic services program, zoning and building control would be used in selected areas to create suitable integrated land-use development by the public or private sector that could be accessed through a voucher system. This would dramatically increase the geographic coverage for affordable urban housing. Those new housing opportunities would be in regulated areas that would provide efficient services combined with urban farming and work center provision. The way this could work is that some private employers could build integrated land use into their campuses for their employees, while public and private developers could provide specialized employment, entrepreneurial and technical services within different housing clusters. The common thread would be the standard housing units and the provision of basic services tailored to different markets. This could greatly improve urban form and allow density to be much more evenly spread since home to work travel would be greatly reduced.

Chapter 13 - The Need for a New Urban Place-Making Paradigm

American society has been continuously changing in response to culture, demographics, technology and environmental factors. At various points in our history there have been good lifestyle features, but almost all of these have lost their luster over time, sometimes to be reclaimed in a different time and circumstance. Barn raisings and square dances served rural and agricultural societies that relied on the seasons and community resources. Family style restaurants worked well when there were plenty of traditional families. Bowling and baseball worked well when people had some kind of basic community and the opportunity for casual social leisure.

In earlier times Americans had comparatively less money and worked long hours, yet when they were free they were truly free for that time. That allowed them to invest more energy and self in leisure activities, and encouraged them to trade and work at local shops and businesses. That was an interrelated organic social and physical environment that had no other purpose than to support the life that surrounded it. At that time main street, school, club and church functioned well as social centers, probably because of a more balanced generational profile, leisure time blocks, and overall social control.

As the Post-World War II baby boom generation came of age with development of suburbs, places like the swimming pool, sports centers, the mall and vacant land became the social focus of young people with less inter-generational interaction, but still with considerable leisure time blocks. These new social locations were separate from other activities and required travel away from the home and neighborhood. Social activities and shopping could be combined at the mall, and sports and social activities at the pool.

There was still some organic character to those environments, but it was limited in time and space because there was less commitment to specific structured activities and frequency of visits.

In very recent times technology has reduced the need to travel to the mall for shopping and social interaction, and sport has continued to degenerate into passive-viewing and techno-fitness which needs no significant common social space and time. More and more all aspects of life are organized according to personal convenience and timing which erode the function of organic interaction. In addition, dramatic socioeconomic changes are taking place within a very short timeframe.

These are: the increase in number of foreign born residents; the urbanization of the country and society, the reduction of traditional home activities such as maintenance; the reduction of organized community activities; the increased role of computers in work and personal activities; the reduced travel needed for many activities; increased small and childless families; increased segregation of the population by education and wealth; decline in support of public schools; reduced association with place and increased mobility; aging of the population and increased separation of demographic groups; political polarization; reduction in unskilled jobs; and broad reduction in middle class prosperity and spending patterns.

All of these changes deserve careful and thorough analysis, especially from the perspective of planning. For the purpose of this book the results of these changes can be noted from anecdotal evidence. There are now few communities that have broad and continuous influence on the American people. Communities are much less physical than ever before and those that exist are being formed in any way, for any purpose, and for any length of time from any resources that are available. As a result, activities and interests are replacing communities as the focus of life attention. This is especially true in younger generations, but is spreading throughout the society and can be given the term, 'ephemeral engagement'.

More free time has been made available as a result of changing lifestyles. Instead of farm, house and yard chores, and community activities, modern Americans have little immediate time commitments beyond work hours. Most passive entertainment and access to information is available at the residence, so eating, drinking and socializing are the primary reasons for public engagement. The emerging gig economy is adding the need for networking and temporary workspace access to these reasons.

Now more after-work time is available than that which is required for eating and drinking, This could be the reason for the upsurge of live entertainment in bars and eateries, although the demise of recorded music sales also plays a part. The success of physical environments is determined by their activity and environmental marketing in order to attract and hold people during their idle time and to get their money. There is no commitment by patrons to any place beyond their immediate satisfaction. Moreover, the limited financial resources of most people restrict the affordability of activities.

The need for lower cost and networked gig-economy workspaces and pop up business spaces has added a new and promising element into the current demands on public space. If we forget about the higher range of shops, eateries and entertainment, and focus on spaces affordable to the majority of people, a new paradigm for place-making might be possible. In order to achieve a more lasting investment in place, a connection between realistic living and working must be developed. Since individual possessions are being reduced, place-making can be achieved by group living and working facilities which have supporting eating, recreation and entertainment spaces. In this scenario we may find that massive investment in public transportation no longer addresses future needs. This type of place-making would put the public sector back in the picture because of its great coordination needs.

The implications of this approach to development are massive - and not only for individual project design, but also for general neighborhood planning. A planning and economic model that integrates the full lifestyle needs of ordinary modern Americans would involve less travel, more shared resources, ease of casual interaction and limited individual investment. This would not necessarily bring back the nostalgic past form of American community, but it would facilitate a place making that is possible for us today and that can create a new national revitalization. As it has been said in the past, "if not us, who? if not now when?"

Development of such place-making neighborhoods to provide full access to affordable space in one package with possible location exchange through linked place memberships - sort of a universal and continuous time-share. This could be possible on an ad hoc and limited basis through existing and emerging mechanisms, and through emerging approaches such as crowd funding. However, the coordination requirements and the need to extend these benefits more broadly to society as a whole strongly suggest that this should be a government or public-private-partnership program implemented through the basic services program. Of course, where there are still employers who require substantial work forces at one site, the private sector can engage in place making for their own employees adjacent to work sites coordinated with public services.

These opportunities for place making for both gig-economy and traditional work places would in themselves reduce the need for travel, transportation and transit. However, the author's research has shown that these new land use influences can only be a minor part of any existing urban region in the short term. In a rapidly growing urban area, it would take about 20 years of substantial and concerted efforts to re-orient land use (essentially forcing all new development to conform to the desired form) in order to have a fundamental impact on transportation. Nevertheless, with major changes in the economy and application in a limited number of power cities, implementation of this new place-making with a basic services program could be implemented with noticeable effect.

If this place-making program is combined with massive deployment of self-driving vehicles that efficiently use spider web-like networks in contrast to corridor-based transit, it will be possible for whatever reduced travel remains in power cities to be more equally distributed. That will present the possibility of both decreased point development density as well as increased general density resulting from the reduction of travel cost obstacles to land development and the associated more efficient development of all urban land.

There are two possible complications to this encouraging scenario: the number of areas of high density development may decrease and present a challenge in providing core infrastructure; and improved vertical transportation technology for elevators and drone-like vehicles may create even higher density in a few areas and challenge the social fabric of power cities by the near complete separation of the power elite and the techno-managerial elite from the mass of the population. The next chapter will present the scenario resulting from the impact of a new transportation system on urban land use.

Chapter 14 - Self-Driving Vehicles and Mobility-Oriented Development

The previous chapter on universal basic services, shared basic services and densified/integrated urban development introduced the concept of a transition from traditional transit to mobility services which would better support the millennial metropolis. Recent and developing technological advances would free urban form and activity patterns from the limited transit corridor and node network, and the private driver-operated vehicle technology that have not been able to bring coherence to most cities. A universal mobility system would respond directly to actual travel demand from new more efficient land use development.

Historical Fixed-Guideway Transit (FGT)

Many professionals, business interests, city boosters, self-anointed opinion leaders and lifestyle mavens promote various urban, social, political and cultural agenda which are not always consistent, even though those agenda are individually attractive or fashionable. The interest in transit, and especially fixed-guideway (FGT) has remained especially popular among urban and transportation planners, despite the generally insurmountable difficulties in development, operation and finance of those systems.

FGT is a concept that has evolved to describe a transit (public people transportation) operation or system layout that is fully contained within a right-of-way where no FGT vehicle is able to operate off the guideway's right-of-way. Often the FGT is underground, but it may be on the surface or elevated. Until recently FGT was confined to various forms of rail operations, but now it also includes roadways which restrict bus operations in the same way: busways, that are different from bus lanes where buses operate on as well as off a right-of-way. FGT really means a transit service that creates a relatively permanent presence in the urban environment, and that reinforces and influences the development and use of nearby land amenities and services to generate large volumes of passengers. A bus lane on the other hand can be cancelled or modified so that adjacent land uses cannot be planned with the assumption of the operational impact of a long-lived facility. In addition, bus lanes can allow bus movement on normal streets for the collection and delivery of passengers in a diffused environment that does not provide the same level of land investment value that can be generated from a FGT station's concentration of movement.

FGT is usually a hoped-for panacea for the urban challenges of traffic congestion, mixed land use development (read: old style main streets but for modern urbanites) and investment instead of decay. More cynically it is often something that transportation and planning professionals would like to have in their technical tool box. The irony in this is that the benefit of FGT stems mainly from its 'fixed' condition and concentrated operation, while the urban environment it serves is un-concentrated. Unfortunately, zoning and building control are generally confined to jurisdictions too small to have significant impact on travel patterns and to have the ability to force concentration of the urban environment. The un-concentrated parts of the urban environment are served largely by private vehicles, with some support from urban bus services. As a compromise, bus lanes have also been introduced. As an effort to reduce the high cost of rail FGT, FGT busways use modified buses, but their rubber tire bus appearance diminishes the public response to that technology in comparison to rail FGT.

Even with the most attractive or most efficient FGT busways it is nearly impossible to create new FGT transit-supporting land uses. This is because a full and balanced loading of the transit vehicles requires corridor focused residential and work location pairs. Land use and transportation accessibility planning practice and research, including that by the author in countries as varied as the United States, India, Pakistan and Kenya, shows that when either part of these pairs is off of the corridor, corridor transit use declines. That has led to a desire to orient both pairs to the corridor, but this is difficult at more than one location due to the weakness of land use control at the metropolitan level. Even when significant quantities of both employment and housing are located on the corridor the chances are limited that these will translate into actual corridor travel pairs because the corridor is only a small part of the metropolitan area and both the employment and housing along it are not restricted pairs; meaning that a resident on the corridor does not necessarily work on it even though he could, and vice versa.

Likely outcomes of government-directed land use and transportation planning are factory town development and corridor-oriented transit-oriented development (TOD). In factory town development, like that of the past, or as found today in countries like China and India (or even American university campuses), where workers live within walking distance of their actual work places, transit use is virtually eliminated, but access to other areas is also limited. In corridor (TOD) development attractive, dense and expensive, but unpaired land uses attract residents or workers who can afford private vehicles to access work and employment opportunities outside the corridor (as evidenced by the retention of private automobiles even in some of the most successful transit corridors such as that in Arlington, Virginia) Well-serviced transit corridors, paradoxically, result in the need for parking space at transit nodes which raises the density and cost of developed sites because the space required for parking is not dedicated to generating and attracting land uses. In some cases the less affluent could be attracted to these higher cost locations if they reallocate their income away from private vehicles, but this would require a remarkable pairing of residence and work on the corridor.

From the above scenario it can be seen that feasible FGT is nearly impossible to create in new urban environments without severe development controls and central planning that has as its goal some sort of FGT corridor with concentrated development (TOD) at only a limited number of mixed land use nodes. For a new system this would normally require almost all future development to be located only at those nodes, leaving the vast majority of metropolitan land outside the nodes at a very low density. That might be an acceptable outcome if people's travel behavior were confined only to matched travel pairs on transit corridors, but there is no assurance of that. If that preferred corridor travel did result, nodal land along the corridors would gain the vast majority of increased metropolitan land values while almost all land outside of the nodes would lose value. Such a situation is especially problematic in today's world where privately-owned real estate is one of the great investment opportunities for most people and where only a few individuals could afford TOD land. Still planners keep working toward the corridor transit model.

On-Demand, Shared and Self-Driving Vehicles

With the advent of coordinated, but un-licensed private vehicle management for mobility services such as Uber, Lyft, etc., and the recent extension of this model to include shared vehicle use offerings, the promise of much more efficient private vehicle operation has been introduced. In that operation the maximum potential mobility is expanded to all origin and destination pairs and the maximum potential efficiency is that of the entire road network capacity. The capacity under that scenario is currently limited by the vehicle size and passenger capacity, and by the road space required for human reaction time. Testing is under way of self-driving vehicles which do not require a driver, but that rely on communications, sensor and artificial intelligence decision-making technology for their operation. These self-driving vehicles have the potential to offer almost unlimited road capacity and demand-responsive operation without the driver cost and space use.

Ownership of shared-use and self-driven vehicles is a subject that has yet been little discussed. Although self-driven vehicles could be trip-maker-owned, few trip-makers are in continuous motion, but only make a few trips per day with the result that the vehicle is in operation for a short part of the day. Mobility service provider-owned vehicles in contrast, could be in nearly continuous operation making the cost per mile or per trip extremely low so that it would be much more efficient for mobility service providers to own the vehicles.

These new technologies and operations offer the potential for high efficiency in urban environments within the road network, with two particular drawbacks - the need for separate drive trains in each vehicle compared to shared drive trains in rail transit, and the less than optimal efficiency of self-driving vehicles operating on roads with traditional human-operated vehicles. Given the vastly greater area covered by roads in comparison to that within FGT corridors, combined with efficient vehicle loading from sophisticated passenger assignment algorithms, the cost of individual drive trains in self-driving vehicles would be more than compensated for by the benefits of the potentially universal origin-destination coverage of the emerging system. That leaves the second drawback of shared individual vehicle operation on roads alongside individual privately-operated vehicles. Although sophisticated shared ride services would certainly offer some improvements over traditional taxis, use of human operators and vehicle operation on roads shared with human operators would greatly reduce the system efficiency because of the need to accommodate less efficient human reaction time.

Today, roadways have capacity limits due mainly to low-occupancy in vehicles, to the interaction with other vehicles at intersections and to the spacing of vehicles to accommodate human reaction.

However, if roadways were used exclusively for self-driving, shared passenger vehicles the roadway space capacity efficiency could be potentially increased toward almost 100 per cent (the amount less than 100% would be due to vehicle non-passenger space and friction at intersections) as a result of more balanced speeds, GPS-linked coordination and almost no reaction time needs. Self-driving vehicles could start and stop at almost every location on the roadway with little friction from other self-driving vehicles because of the GPS navigation system movement optimization. In order to achieve the technical operations potential of self-driving vehicles, human-operated vehicles would have to be removed from the urban road system.

The greater the density, number and road network of trips, the greater would be the potential to assign passengers efficiently to vehicles. The efficiency of FGT is only along its right-of-way and for the parts of the origin-destination travel that are contained within its corridor - or more precisely, between corridor station nodes. Outside of those corridors, trips must be performed or completed by non-FGT vehicles. Even trips within the FGT corridor itself may be diverted to self-driving vehicles as a result of their more flexible schedules. When all trips can be more densely loaded and routed on the entire roadway network, there would be no need for corridor FGT for the vast majority of all trips, except between dense nodes in low density environments. The potential to remove FGT corridor transit services would withdraw an expensive capital and operations cost from urban government general budgets, and transfer the full cost of mobility to the users and the profit to private mobility service operators. Mobility would be greatly increased, and the current public subsidy to transit and private vehicle capital and operations would also be removed, requiring a new regime to ensure equity of access.

Smart Cities and Urban Total System Management

From this analysis it becomes clear that the goal of the promoters of self-driving vehicles is to establish a new transportation and mobility system composed of self-driving vehicles and the supporting operational system often termed the Internet of Things (IoT). To achieve that, the main challenges will be to develop the IoT, impose control over the road network, remove private, human-driven vehicles and allow only self-driving vehicles connected to the new vehicle operation system to use the road network. Achieving this scale of system change would seem to be a tall order. However, 100 years ago there were many animals and animal-drawn vehicles on city streets, yet those disappeared within a very few years. Already there are extensive vehicle restrictions on roadways, such as on those for high-occupancy and bus lanes, so the changes needed may not be significantly more challenging.

All self-driving vehicles would need to be linked to a common GPS navigation system and the vehicle operational system would also have to be common. Even vehicle size and performance specifications would best be standardized for the navigational system to coordinate. The same would be true for road and intersection design and regulation. In addition, sensors, traffic control devices and the central smart city control system would have to be fully compatible with all the above.

It is highly unlikely that local governments could operate and manage so much integration and standardization in light of the general failure of metropolitan scale planning and systems operation. However, that failure is largely due to the nature of jurisdictional government. Non-jurisdictional systems providers on the other hand, such as Google, Microsoft, Amazon and Facebook, have managed to succeed in spanning their standardized control across almost all jurisdictions. What they have not demonstrated yet is the extension of this control to ubiquitous physical assets that operate within jurisdictions, although they are trying to achieve this in innovative ways. Ultimately standardized cyber-technology could be transferred to self-driving vehicles and systems that have no relationship with or need for jurisdictions; but only need standardization, operational freedom and unified systems.

A physical network for mobility is already present in the form of roads, which would not have to be assembled piecemeal, whose ownership is almost exclusively public and for which there are no private claims. That space has some similarity to air space, except that roads and the origins and destinations they lead to are fixed on the ground. The challenge of implementing a new mobility system can best be understood by a consideration of the system components and the current operators/regulators which are presented below:

	System Component	Operator/Regulator
1.	road and intersection design and operations	governments
2.	traffic control devices	governments
3.	enforcement	governments
4.	GPS navigation	commercial providers
5.	smart city sensors and monitoring	commercial providers, private operators, governments
6.	data base and computer operating systems	commercial providers
7.	vehicles	all users public and private, governments
8.	vehicle design and performance	commercial providers, all users public and private, governments

All the above would need to be perfectly coordinated for the system to work. It would be challenging for governments to combine the above components and fit them together to the precision necessary for the envisaged mobility system, especially considering the speed with which technology is currently advancing. Operation by technical government entities such as NASA, would also be possible, but is unlikely due to the current advanced development of specific technologies and vehicles by the private sector. Although it is conceptually possible for individual components and locations to be operated by different entities, the additional coordination of these would be challenging and costly.

That would suggest private monopoly operation and maintenance of the entire system - even the roads which have heretofore been largely in the public domain. A long-term leasing or concession arrangement subject to government oversight would allow the deployment of unified systems with required maintenance ensured by the operator. This would also provide an answer to the difficulties that local government has in maintaining roads and other related infrastructure. If a long-term lease or concession arrangement were adopted some sort of utility regulatory structure would be needed mainly to ensure fair pricing, proper operations and conformity with various standards and regulations. Moreover, due to the likely proprietary nature of operational software, vehicles and supporting equipment, it is unlikely that the initial system operator would ever be replaced.

The mobility system operator would also need wide regulation and enforcement power to ensure that the system operation is not compromised. This would be especially noticeable on roads where only use by the operator would be allowed, which would eventually be all roads. That would prohibit human-operated vehicles initially from priority roads in power cities, and then rapidly extend restrictions to most power city roads in order to accommodate the efficiency needs of the investors and system operators. Accompanying this, the benefits of giving up private vehicles would need to be widely promoted and initially subsidized such as was done in the 'cash for clunkers' program or by tight control of mobility charges.

Installation of increasingly sophisticated electronics in private vehicles and installation of electronics throughout the urban system are well under way providing the initial input to the new mobility system. An example of this type of system is the growing worldwide lobby for 'smart cities'. So-called smart city planning for city-wide integration of urban activities and services would initially entail the extensive installation of sensors, monitors and devices to efficiently link and monitor individuals, locations and behavior. The most well-known example of this is in the core City of London area where there is almost complete monitoring of movements for security purposes. Beyond security, sensors, monitors and devices can also collect real-time, detailed and comprehensive information at the individual level about service demand and consumption.

In providing the potential for ultimate efficiency, the mobility system would calculate specific charges for each individual at each time for each trip, reflecting the actual cost of service. This type of system has already been partially introduced through cell phone and ISP linkage with GPS tracking. This system would specifically calculate and apply real time user charges through a universal individual identification and monitoring system. Individual identification numbers connected to a database could also be used to apply subsidies such as for senior citizens, children, unemployed, the physically challenged, etc. The current transportation system imposes charges in various unconnected and indirect ways such as property taxes, gas tax, tolls, and ticketing, which separate capital, maintenance, operations costs and policy-based fare and access charges, distorting the perception of cost by making the actual cost of travel very different from the charge paid. The new mobility system could introduce a more transparent combined cost-based charge which would be a major change from the current travel pricing regime.

In addition, the smart city system would be used to capture revenues automatically and without the need for traditional human monitoring, enforcement and collection. Under this system debiting could be made in real-time from the designated source of funds. Anyone who has received an automated camera-generated speeding ticket has experienced the first stage of this automated and anonymous system. The next stage would be direct debiting rather than an indirect bill.

It should be noted that the specific use of the smart city IoT in this discussion is for the mobility system. The majority of travel is work- and subsistence-related and so is unavoidable and largely involuntary. Management and operation of this system would provide the opportunity to charge a monopoly profit for a large part of human endeavor. Moreover, there would be little to stop its intrusion into all other sectors of life. As a result, the new mobility system is almost certain to become a regulated monopoly by jurisdiction if not by larger geographic region. This new transportation system is likely to resemble the regulated cable TV monopoly on steroids. Even with price regulation, the scale of the system is so large that the profits on individual components and on such a large part of human endeavor may dwarf all other investment opportunities. Moreover, since this new system would have major urban development, services, finance and consumption impacts, the additional and likely unregulated potential economic and political power to be derived cannot yet be imagined or overstated.

Self-driving vehicles would initially and mainly be in power cities because of jurisdictional, travel density and cost reasons for the same reasons that cable TV and high speed Internet have not yet reached many non-urban areas of the country. The necessary driver-operated vehicles in suburban and rural areas (where travel to individual destinations could not be easily grouped) would ultimately face restrictions to their operation within urban areas, requiring transfers from non-urban to urban transportation systems, and even incurring urban entry charges.

Moreover, the current road infrastructure finance model is likely to change as control over an increasing portion of the transportation infrastructure is transferred to commercial operators and its associated costs charged directly to users. That would almost certainly mean the removal of gas tax and even property tax from urban mobility funding. Since urban mobility system users would be paying the direct costs for their mobility, they would likely object to subsidizing the huge portion of the national transportation infrastructure outside of urban mobility systems which would then have to be supported by much higher gas taxes, property taxes or tolls in non-urban areas.

The likelihood of this change taking place has already been suggested by the recent increase in professional discussions of introducing vehicle mile traveled (VMT) charges on the shared road infrastructure for private road users rather than or in addition to using a common gas tax fund. Support for this approach will grow as more electric vehicles are introduced and the collection of gas tax decreases. This support is understandable since the administrative class is now more urban than it was a generation ago and more willing to impose new charges on less-affluent, non-urban and private car-owning families that they do not identify with. Ultimately this could provoke political opposition, increased migration to efficient urban areas or both.

The Need for Mobility-Oriented Development

The establishment of separate urban and non-urban mobility systems would at some point be intolerable for the suburban and rural populations who would be forced to lower their standards of living space and independence. For some, this could be facilitated by a priority program to make urban density affordable to them. One way to achieve this is through the greater use of vertical space, shared living and working facilities, etc. Even in his Plan Voisin for the early motor age in Paris 100 years ago, le Corbusier envisaged more efficient cities with shared child care, recreation and open space, and in vertical separation of activities, so making cities more affordable should not be beyond the imagination today.

Perhaps, the necessary form of future urban development would be more like that of Doxiadis' Ekistics model than like the traditional modernism of le Corbusier. Doxiadis envisaged the ultimate meeting of all urban neighborhoods and settlements as conglomerations. While some shared services such as fire, police, shopping and recreation may necessitate some degree of urban density clusters, the need for high density nodes to support FGT would fade away. As a result, the currently fashionable, but expensive and difficult to achieve transit-oriented development (TOD) model would rapidly disappear from the planner's toolkit. In its place would be development at densities and concentrations driven by other social, economic and financial forces, and a new paradigm would be established - *mobility-oriented development (MOD)*.

Even in this predicted radical change for future mobility and urban development, historical patterns will remain. In some ways the future is likely to present a return to earlier more energy efficient urban patterns that existed before the automobile and street car eras. The underlying force behind these changes - beyond technology - is the impact of a decline in standards of living. At the same time that mobility is increased for most of the population, some forms of freedom and affordability of the new urban environment will be reduced.

Self-driving vehicles, changing urban form and smart city management will introduce an urban planning environment that phases out traditional transit service, greatly expands the use of technology and personal information, and confirms the use and regulation of integrated larger scale urban development and service provision. The result will be the need for increased understanding of how the relationship between technology and human activity is managed increasingly through public-private partnerships. This will be far different from the historical transportation and urban planning experience.

The requirements of efficient self-driving vehicle and smart city electronic control systems highlight the disparity between advanced and less developed areas and countries. Moving from an environment of uncoordinated and independent urban service users and activity locations to one of system level monitoring, management and control is a civilizational change due to the combined presence of technological capacity, wealth and coercive power of government which was not possible previously. Now it may become possible in developed countries, but not in less developed countries. However, even in developed countries the complications of imposing smart city management on the increasingly stratified power cities will be a great challenge because it will involve a reduction in standard of living and freedom for many. This challenge will be met with some combination of universal basic services and personal electronic identification. The cost of urban services will increasingly be imposed on users automatically either through a basic services program or through automatic charges, which will be difficult to impose without significant political resistance.

The increased mobility, scale of management, and loss of freedom that will be caused by the self-driving vehicle system's ultimate operation will primarily be experienced in advanced and wealthy power cities. The less developed cities and non-urban areas will not be able to introduce the same level of operation because of management and financial constraints associated with the mobility system that is foreseen for developed cities, although much less efficient self-driving operations may be possible in mixed road operation alongside human-driven vehicles. In light of the increasing trend toward income disparities throughout the world it is likely that a combination of spatial stratification and special roads for the rich and powerful will emerge in less developed cities. In developed cities, spatial stratification by income is also expected to increase and mobility stratification is likely to be achieved by vertical means such as Elon Musk's Hyperloop, and personal drone-type vehicles that avoid interaction with ground and horizontal movement.

Chapter 15 - The Emerging New Urban Political Economy

The previous chapters have explored the economic and social changes that are taking place to create an increasingly urbanized world, with a limited number of power cities controlling the other cities and non-urban areas. Even within the power cities, the stratification of wealth and power is moving toward an unsustainable conclusion where urban services cannot be provided at a common standard under the current political economy. Concentrations of activities within urban areas such as were experienced in the past and supported traditional urban transit services are in general decline. Self-driving vehicle mobility services will support and encourage dense but disbursed development patterns that are less efficient to serve with urban infrastructure, but which are more affordable for individual households. Some bastions of intense vertical development continue to remain and expand for powerful institutions and wealthy individuals who will take advantage of new technologies to avoid mass ground transportation in accessing their destinations.

For the majority of urban residents this emerging environment will be fraught with challenges and insecurity if urban form is shaped in an ad hoc manner without strong guidance toward an efficient outcome. Normal market forces will not provide this efficiency and government intervention will be required. A basic urban services program as the foundation for urban planning and operations would respond to the changing urban economy and the need for improved efficiency in order to provide a common basic level of services.

What would be social and governance implications of such a basic services program? First and foremost, this program would require a new social contract that commits all members of society to paying for and supporting common urban services on a permanent basis. This would ultimately have to be done through government facilitation. Since some members cannot pay their cost of the common services, a basic urban services program would have to do so. Of course, funds for basic urban services could not come from thin air. They would have to come from the wealthier part of the population. Agreed services would be guaranteed which would resolve one source of great social dispute. Continuous budget battles, neglect of public assets, inferior services, public dissatisfaction and inequities, etc. would be greatly reduced or eliminated.

Of course, this does mean that all people will lose some freedom. That is not philosophically attractive, but it is necessary as part of a new social contract. Since the government as the executive for implementation of the social contract will ensure the capacity of all citizens to comply with standards through the basic services program, it will also acquire the right of regulation. That can be dangerous and must be carefully controlled. One of the key issues that has obstructed many urban development and management plans is that of public behavior. In American society relocation and exclusion have increasingly been the only recourse for anyone who is not happy with the behavior of others. This cannot continue. With a basic services program some freedoms may also be affected such as location and behavior. That is the cost of the new social contract which would be binding on all citizens.

What impact would this program of basic services have on urban form and the urban political economy? To start with this does not necessarily mean the creation of an egalitarian society. Of course, in recent years the current economic structure has pushed and will continue to push more and more people into the fragile working class. There is an increasing techno-managerial class as well as a power elite. Those two classes would continue to enjoy a privileged status in the economy, but that status would be reduced in order to pull the working class back up into a more stable middle class. This would not be the middle class of the 1950s because that was never sustainable, but it would be a new economy urban middle class with more shared resources, less daily travel, more local orientation and more security than today. It would be in large part a return to a medieval urban form of political economy.

The implementation of an urban basic services program requires a comprehensive approach and is not simply a wealth redistribution activity. In particular it requires comprehensive planning to coordinate area developments and maximize shared facilities and urban infrastructure. Although it is urgently needed, it is likely to take years to implement through an incremental approach. During this time, considerable existing and ongoing development will remain. In particular this will include the segregation of the power elite and techno-managerial class from the majority of urban residents. This will be achieved in part by some of the projects of Elon Musk such as the Hyperloop and the Boring Company. Can both urban basic services and segregation of the wealthy from the masses continue side by side. Can each group tolerate the other, and for how long?

Chapter 16 - The Way Forward

The current power city phenomenon cannot continue for long. Every economy and society must ultimately have a basic stability. Today, all trends are working against that stability and leading toward social conflict. The preceding chapters have narrated recent trends in political economy and especially rapid developments in technology. The key points to address are:

- evolution of cities as the dominant forces in human ecology
- changes in technology, economic structures and massive population sizes that have produced a new techno-managerial class and diminished the power of the Great American Middle Class
- reduction in the need for production labor and the widening gap between highly skilled and routine professional skills
- emergence of a limited number of power cities that dominate the other cities and non-urban areas
- a global political economy that drives activities and systems that make power cities and the techno-managerial elite of different nations more alike, and those within nations less alike
- the alliance of the techno-managerial elite with the downtrodden classes
- modern economy, communications, education, business, government and security systems that are dominated by immigrants, the footloose, ethnic and lifestyle minorities, and the education and cultural elite, who use the downtrodden classes as their tools to dominate a declining Great American Middle Class
- power cities and techno-managerial elites seeking to bypass their hinterlands and nation states to establish independent relationships with the global political economy

- changes in the spatial dimension of human activities away from the nodal concentrations of the industrial age to highly disbursed, ubiquitous and cyber activities that challenge centralized infrastructure systems
- emergence of new technologies, economic information systems and platforms, IoT/smart cities, etc. that allow full knowledge, monitoring, and control of urban man
- increasing and high cost of housing and infrastructure in urban areas and especially in power cities
- price distortions in urban land due to limited transportation infrastructure and capacity, zoning/building control, demographic settlement patterns, security, lack of behavior control and poor home and work land use linkages
- emergence of decentralized mobility services that will make possible nearly any locations for home and work
- the reduction in standard of living and general wealth that requires reduced possessions and consumption, especially of space and privacy

Additional issues that emerge from this environment are:

- diverging standards of living, financial security, career opportunities, lifestyle preferences, etc., among age cohorts possibly leading to intergenerational conflict
- standard of living gaps and technology gaps, particularly between power cities and the rest, that make it difficult to sustain freedom of movement between jurisdictions
- potential for new technology to separate the power elite and techno-managerial elite from the rest by vertical means such as Hyperloop, advanced elevators and large drone vehicles
- both increased and decreased density patterns. In many locations spot density will be decreased or restrained as a result of much more accessible land area with the use of self-driving vehicles and on-demand mobility services. Increased

overall density will be as a result of monopoly of amenities and opportunities in power cities, vertical transportation technology and exclusive lifestyle preference, and more efficient land access (development of land at lower density that would otherwise have been left undeveloped)

The above conditions define the possibilities for global urban settlement. Earlier four possible outcomes were presented and are again given here:

1. modern urban world development is reversed by population reduction, reducing the demand for services
2. a two or three tier service level system is introduced that allows the most basic - but not the desired - services in urban infrastructure to be provided in all urban settlements, but allows higher standards of services to be isolated for the remaining middle class, and for the techno-managerial and power elite class
3. all citizens are allowed to choose where and how they live with no certainty or standard of municipal services, and ultimately requiring local area and private arrangement of services - this would be the current state experienced in less developed countries combined with the almost certain segregation of elites from the rest of the population
4. common services are provided as municipal monopolies for all of a single class of citizens only in approved and viable urban settlements where they are efficient and affordable, while guaranteed municipal services to other urban areas are phased out - the Millennial Metropolis Model (MMM).

The previous chapters have covered two main themes: the current trend of decline for the Great American Middle Class and the emergence of a new techno-managerial elite and the widening gap between the two in the context of political economy; and the need for and possibilities of more dense, cooperative and shared community living in urban areas. The two themes do not at first seem to be compatible, particularly because the first is discouraging for most people, while the second is objectively encouraging.

The second theme is the urban development that is associated with the preferred MMM outcome above. That theme has been presented as a possibility rather than an established reality such as the dominance of the political economy by the techno-managerial elite. The MMM requires a common standard of municipal services across all classes for development in only specified areas while public services in other areas are phased out. This means that in the areas with phased out services those who can afford to provide for themselves may do so. However, the cost would be high so only a small number could afford this. In the areas with public services of a common standard the residents could still represent a wide range of wealth. Providing common basic services would require a minimum density which could accommodate the rich or non-rich.

Basic services include housing and, especially in power cities, currently have a high cost. This is normally perceived as a high cost of housing, but this is misleading. Henry George in the mid-1800s had an understanding of the nature of urban land and building values. As he explained, the land component is the most buoyant because it is a result of increasing urban population and infrastructure improvements. Buildings are materials and labor based and are depreciating assets. He argued that land is a public asset and should be rented to users while buildings are privately owned. So the high cost of power city housing is due to a large and affluent population and the value of infrastructure. Population as well as overall wealth is certain to continue growing along with the value of infrastructure so the unit cost of housing cannot come down in its current form.

Instead, the consumption of housing in space and infrastructure would have to be reduced in order to reduce the unit cost. This can be accomplished with the MMM where the size of housing and consumption of infrastructure services would be reduced in part through the sharing of facilities to reduce duplication and waste. Moreover, development would only be supported where infrastructure services could be provided efficiently, such as along main water lines, rather than at remote locations. That would allow city administration to provide basic services at the lowest unit cost. The basic services program as described earlier would not be charged to the basic users. Wealthier users to the extent that they desire to enjoy greater space and consume more service units, but locate where basic services can be provided efficiently, would pay for that above and beyond the standard basic services package. Of course, the more affluent would also be paying part of the cost of the basic services for all through general taxation.

Two questions arise with regard to this proposal. The first is how much the wealth of the affluent would be reduced as a result of providing subsidies to those whose contribution to general taxation do not meet the cost of basic services, and how well they would accept this. The second is how much greater would the consumption of the affluent remain and how acceptable this would be to the general public. These calculations would require our best minds and considerable time. However, this would present a reasonable possibility of compromise between the two broad groups.

This would address the increasing difficulty of a large part of the population to make ends meet as a result of income inequality, and also provide peace of mind in the face of increasing automation threats to job security. Addressing these two issues would go a long way toward ensuring social stability within the power city. In principle there would still be the opportunity for middle class, the techno-managerial elite and even the power elite to earn and spend more than a large part of the population, however, that amount would be restrained by the shared cost of providing universal basic services.

This structure would almost certainly narrow the currently wide gap between the power elite and the techno-managerial elite, and the rest. That is a good thing, but would that also achieve the additional need to re-integrate the power and techno-managerial elites with the broader society economically, socially and politically? Conceptually residential locations of the elite and the rest of the population would be separate due to the nature of their income and consumption even if these were reduced by the costs of the universal basic services program. Moreover, if there remains a substantial income gap between the elites and the other classes, income segregation is bound to result in part because modern technology is increasingly providing opportunity for income segregation. Some income segregation for various reasons is natural, but when it becomes so great that there is no common interest it is not socially sustainable.

Excessive income segregation can be avoided if it is within localities or communities rather than between different communities. Universal basic services would discourage income segregation between communities because services would be common and not determined by property taxes. This would result in a settlement pattern more like that in Nordic countries than that currently prevalent in the United States and most of the rest of the world.

It is necessary to roll back the current informal eugenics that has been most effectively identified by Charles Murray through which the techno-managerial class is increasingly isolating itself from the rest of the population through education, marriage and related grouping among elites. The first step in addressing this problem is to re-establish the role and use of public education as a shared infrastructure by among income groups. Because of declining employment opportunities in the new economy there will be more emphasis on broader aspects of education rather than only on techno-managerial professions. Combined with proximate living of the more affluent with ordinary people, more balanced and re-oriented education should help to reduce dual super-professional households, the current unsustainable social distance, and the size of income and wealth gaps. Moreover, guaranteed basic services and more equitable income distribution should also reduce the winner take all mentality and restore recently lost social stability, community loyalty and commitment, and institutional memory.

The MMM would be oriented to nodal development, but nodal development that is based on efficient infrastructure provision and is largely self-oriented with integrated residence, work, services and shopping. For implementing the MMM nodal development would initially take place at existing locations that are well served by existing infrastructure. As the model is extended to the entire urban area new nodes may be developed that can be efficiently connected to the main infrastructure systems. At some point the nodes that can be efficiently connected to the main systems will be exhausted and options for the remaining areas will be less efficient local, independent infrastructure, or dedication as open space or other less intensive uses.

One slightly tricky issue is that of domicile mobility - or, the ability to live wherever one wants to. Normally this does not arise within the nation-state, although the cases of the Soviet Union, South Africa and China have had restrictions on this, and other states may use administrative deterrents rather than restrictions. However, there has been little debate on the issue of entitlements and obligations based on domicile, particularly in the United States. As discussed earlier, residents of any given place at any given time were able to participate through the political process in the long term planning and financial commitments of local urban governments. However, their financial participation was limited to annual taxes or possibly only daily taxes. This meant that someone could vote for a long term bond and the next day leave for another place with lower taxes, leaving the city of origin with population minus one to cover the cost, and adding one new demand to the population of the destination city with pre-existing capacity.

In a time of population and economic growth this action may have made no difference. However, in the modern age of power cities, production and returns to labor is not able to cover the costs of basic services. Even with significant contribution from the owners of capital it may still not be possible if service cost and finance are restricted to each jurisdiction. Almost certainly a universal basic service policy would have to be based on some degree of national equity, so that costs in each city would be covered by national revenues rather than by local revenues. Although efficiency would be a high priority, cities losing population and cities gaining population may experience unequal increases in cost for providing basic services that can only be balanced at the national level since domicile mobility is a national facility.

Of course, the alternative to this is to restrict mobility, but that would inevitably mean the walling off of power cities from the rest of the country which would be in opposition to the goal to reduce the social and economic inequalities caused by the emergence of power cities. In short, people from outside power cities should have the opportunity to settle there to the extent that the required efficient development for basic service provision can be provided so that the current residents do not establish a monopoly on the national opportunities there. This approach might suggest that ultimately most people will migrate to power cities. Although this is a possibility, it would take a long time and might never happen; however, a substantial move will take place, but it will be reduced when most people have security of basic services in other places as well - without the requirement of employment. Movement from place to place within nation states would be limited by the MMM capacity of each city. MMM development can be provided in second tier cities and towns, as well as the hinterland also since basic services would also be provided there and would ensure the viability of living in those places even with the current power city dominance.

The long term goal of national equity and social peace will ultimately require some dispersion of activities away from the power cities. Although this is a long-term goal it should be started soon as part of the MMM. Since nodal development will be oriented to co-located employment and housing, dispersion of power city activities should be part of a national planning process. One key objective to be achieved is to avoid the major relocation of established power city elites to secondary cities and towns to take advantage of new opportunities there. New opportunities should generally be restricted to existing residents and their capacity should be built as part of that process. Most importantly, the present obsession with extant so-called merit must be dispensed with in favor of national and local capacity development. It is time to begin the process of comprehensively upgrading national human resources, rather than manipulating populations from place to place to serve the needs of capital.

Upgrading national human resources rather than continued concentration of opportunities for the techno-managerial elite and the knowledge class will be a key element of the MMM. This can initially be facilitated by new more objective and transparent hiring and selection procedures on merit to the extent possible, and combined with the extension of anti-trust and anti-conflict of interest actions to level the playing field for all, particularly for local talent to compete. That approach would be based on the concept of maximum utilization and opportunity for the local population. Thus localization can be considered as a plank of the MMM.

With the introduction of universal basic services the cost of all members of society to the nation would be clearly, directly and fully felt by the nation. That cost would not only include recurring costs, but also the fixed infrastructure costs including education, government, public facilities, national infrastructure, etc. The MMM implies the reduction of ownership by a few, particularly of technology platforms, in favor of citizen shareholdership. With this understanding it would be difficult to justify any but the most exceptional immigration until the native-born population is developed to the maximum. Even then immigration would imply a market transaction of paid admission to the national universal basic services system.

Some would say that the MMM approach is too radical, ambitious and utopian. To the contrary, human and American history is filled with similar visions and efforts. What is different about our time is that popular vision has become both defeatist and limited in thinking that achieving solutions to present problems is too much effort on top of the unexpected and increasing struggles for daily survival . The current trend of domination by power cities and the techno-managerial elite is already threatening what is left of the hope for daily survival as we can see from the not very attractive other three urbanization alternatives which are equally possible as the MMM. Moreover, individual freedom has already been reduced and will continue to be reduced as a result of urbanization under any scenario.

The defeatist outlook has spread from the general public even to activists and professionals. Many think that they can't affect their environments and future, and that they have to accept the conditions and limitations that are imposed on them through the techno-managerial elite. For example, for any ambitious program like the MMM, visionary and energetic planners are needed to address multi-disciplinary issues. Yet, public sector planners have in recent times surrendered the leadership of urban planning to a plethora of private sector developers with limited vision and focus on market profit. That is unsustainable.

Now is the time for the public sector to reassert its leading role in urban planning, political economy and multi-sector coordination. The MMM will require both urban and regional planning; intensive place-making for each node; coordination of employment, business incubation and entrepreneurial development space; of market services with the private sector; and of infrastructure systems and service planning. This cannot be done by individual developers or even by planners at even the power city level alone. This must be taken up at the national level in the manner of major public works, wartime mobilization and New Deal programs.

The MMM requires an understanding of the new urbanized world whose conditions are no longer categorized by old political definitions. Power cities, and the power and techno-managerial elite that control them are the fundamental political economy reality in the Age of Trump and managing them requires a new social contract rather than mere electoral musical chairs. The Millennial Metropolis Mode is the successor to Doxiadis' ekistics; is now and is the future.

References

1. Gibbons, H.T. Scott (2016). <u>Trapped by History: The Remaking of America and Death of the Middle Class</u>. Amazon.

2. Piketty, Thomas (2014) <u>Capital in the Twenty-First Century</u>. Harvard University Press.

3. Murray, Charles (2012). <u>Coming Apart: The State of White America</u>. Crown Forum.

4. Bookchin, Murray (1987). <u>The Rise of Urbanization and the Decline of Citizenship</u>. Sierra Club Books.

5. Fukuyama, Francis (2006). <u>The End of History and the Last Man</u>. Free Press.

6. Naim, Moses (2013). <u>The End of Power: From Boardrooms to Battlefields and Churches to States, Why Being in Charge Isn't What it Used to Be</u>. Basic Books.

7. Turchin, Peter (2016). <u>Ages of Discord</u>. Beresta Books.

8. von Thünen (1966). <u>von Thünen's Isolated State: An English Addition</u>. Pergamon.

9. Ahmed, Nafeez (2017). <u>Failing States, Collapsing Systems: BioPhysical Triggers of Political Violence</u>. Springer Briefs in Energy.

10. le Corbusier (2017). <u>The City of Tomorrow and Its Planning</u>. Dover Publications (Reissue).

11. George, Henry (2013). <u>Progress and Poverty</u>. Robert Schalkenbach Foundation.

12. Doxiadis, Constantinos (1968). <u>Ekistics: An Introduction to the Science of Human Settlements</u>. Oxford University Press.